I Can Do This

The Bloody Mary Story

Bobbie Weiner

with Stephanie Allmon

AuthorHouse™
1663 Liberty Drive
Bloomington, IN 47403
www.authorhouse.com
Phone: 1-800-839-8640

First published by AuthorHouse 6/24/2011

ISBN: 978-1-4634-0788-9 (e)
ISBN: 978-1-4634-0789-6 (dj)
ISBN: 978-1-4634-0787-2 (sc)

Library of Congress Control Number: 2011907671

Printed in the United States of America

Any people depicted in stock imagery provided by Thinkstock are models,
and such images are being used for illustrative purposes only.
Certain stock imagery © Thinkstock.

This book is printed on acid-free paper.

For Sol

Contents

Forward

By Tom Carlton

I met Bobbie in October of 2001. I know that because 9/11 just happened about one month prior to meeting her.

I was working in an aggressive print shop that had a quick turn-around and was always growing. In fact it was growing to the point that what I did there was becoming obsolete. I was a graphic artist who did the prepress work; you know, the "paste up" artist. And with computer expansion, my position was dissolving. So I was kind a stuck in a hard place. My job was going to end — that much was certain — and yes, I could have moved on to different areas in the print shop, but I knew in my heart I wanted to stay with art.

So I started work on a comic book — one that I myself would find a way to publish and distribute; easier said than done. But I was committed to the idea, so I worked at it night and day and my efforts to finish the book paid off. Of course, not the way I was expecting it to. I was very close to the end of the project when my life would change forever.

Bobbie came into the print shop one morning in October of 2001 and while she was getting some copies made, she casually asked the woman at the counter if she knew of an artist who could do comic books. The print shop worker, of course, knew about my book and informed her that the artist who worked there was, in fact, working on one. So she took down her number and gave it to me.

At first I hesitated to call, as I wanted to finish my comic book and see what I could do with it, but my more practical side (my wife Ellen) informed me that I should call her and see what she had in mind. So

I called, and over the weekend I met her at her office. She hired me as a freelance artist to draw "Tales of Bloody Mary" after I showed her my comic book. The first year was a bit rough, as I still worked at the print shop and did the art from home. But almost one year to the date, I finalized my job at the print shop and after 14 years there, came on to work with Bobbie to live out my dream.

It's not often that one actually gets that opportunity to live out a dream, but I have and it's all because Bobbie is a driven woman with passion for what she does. I have never met anyone with this much drive. It's like she sees what needs to happen and does it no matter what it takes. I have been to two Comic-Cons in San Diego and many other events and conventions. I have been blessed with a fun job and great boss. It's not unlike being on Bobbie's surf board while she rides the tidal wave of success that she has created.

To further illustrate this, I'm reminded of a story she once told me about her childhood at the beach. As a child she would collect large abalone shells and paint them. Then she would sell them as ashtrays to people as they walked around down by the beach… even as a young child she was already driven to succeed. I find that speaks volumes as to who she really is.

I have known Bobbie for almost a decade at the time of this writing and have seen my dream grow and change along the way. Not many people get that chance to live out a dream, but I have and it's due to a remarkable woman named Bobbie Weiner. I could go on and on about how many wonderful things she has done, but it would take volumes to write it all out. She is the best in so many ways.

Chapter 1

'Just Like Hollywood'

Sitting on the edge of our bed as he dressed for work one morning, my husband of nine years looked me in the face and delivered the news that would shake my otherwise perfect life to the core in ways so profound, I would feel the aftershocks for years to come.

"You are my best friend and I love you, but I want my life to be just like Hollywood — like the soap operas," he said matter-of-factly. "I want a divorce."

I was so dumbstruck, I couldn't force out words — not even an argument.

The man of my dreams was telling me he had a new dream for himself. And, as he approached his 50th birthday on this day in 1992, his new happily-ever-after didn't include me. The magical, fairy-tale existence I'd been living with my plastic surgeon-husband in Los Angeles was over in the millisecond it took him to say the four words, "I want a divorce."

He left for work as usual — sure, his day would go along just as he'd planned.

I, on the other hand, could hardly get my brain to switch on. I stumbled to a phone and forced my fingers to dial the first person I could think of — my husband's mother. She and I had always been close — surely she could convince him to change his mind and come back, right? She was just as shocked as I was when I broke the news, but ultimately she was his mother, and she felt like she had to support him.

I thought about my own parents, Sol and Betty, married for decades, living a happy life together and growing old together in Florida. I couldn't bring myself to call them on this unspeakably hurtful morning; not yet. They would be too disappointed in the daughter they doted on. The daughter who, after some rough years, had a seemingly perfect life as The Doctor's Wife now.

"A perfect life as The Doctor's Wife." That's sure what it looked like from the outside in.

Just two days earlier, we'd returned from a glorious week on the ski slopes of Colorado. We owned a great house in Bel Air, kept a gorgeous boat at Marina Del Ray and had a garage filled with sports cars. Our neighbors were movie stars; our friends were movers and shakers. I got to spend my days playing tennis at the country club, and my nights at glitzy fundraisers for the children's hospital.

But more important than all those material riches was the fact that I had become a dutiful stepmom to my husband's little boy — a boy who was now a teenager and a handful, but who I loved as though he were my own flesh and blood.

I had adored my husband and had been his biggest fan for nine years. He was a marvelous, funny guy who'd provided so much for me, and for whom I'd sacrificed so much.

Just a few years earlier, I'd rearranged my whole life to help him through his recovery from alcohol and drug addiction. I'd been his rock. I'd been there for him when he was drinking three bottles of vodka a day. I'd been there for him when he was stealing Xanax from the hospital and downing liquid cocaine like it was Diet Coke. I'd been there for him when he fell down during surgery and the hospital called me to come get him.

Every day during his recovery, I would get up and go to the hospital and eat breakfast with him for 15 minutes at 6:30 in the morning. And when he went back to work, I'd sit in the parking garage underneath the hospital and wait for him all day — he said he just needed to know I was there.

And now, this. THIS! A divorce? How dare he?

I'd never doubted my husband's feelings for me. Had I been delusional, or had he been a great actor?

This was the marriage that was going to stick, I had decided. I was no stranger to divorce. I had been married before. Three times, in fact — short-lived marriages that never really "launched" in the first place. But this was the one that was going to go the distance. This was the fairytale ending my mother dreamed for me since I was a little girl, the product of two deliriously happy, married parents.

This man was THE ONE.

Except now, he wasn't.

THE ONE had taken a gun to my life and shot my heart, and I was quite sure that if anyone came looking, they would find pieces of it all over Los Angeles.

The "soap opera" my husband had crafted for himself, I soon discovered, included a 19-year-old girlfriend, a heroin addict in Venice Beach. He and his son — now almost a grown man himself — packed up and left me. My stepson sold all the furniture so he, too, could fund a drug habit.

I'd been cut from this family's script a long time ago, but I was the last to know.

My husband literally rode off on his Harley into the California sunset.

He got his wish: a scene straight out of Hollywood.

അ അ അ അ അ

The emptiness of having lost my two best friends, my husband and my stepson, felt utterly agonizing. My husband quickly erased me from his world without a second thought, as if I had become a burden that cramped his hot new lifestyle.

Confronted with a decade of memories, I saw only one choice: I left the house of my dreams, disposed of whatever I had left and faced the fact that, at age 46, I was now a living, breathing Hollywood cliché: a middle-age woman abandoned by her rich husband, without her own money, career or backup plan.

Nothing was left of my perfect life as The Doctor's Wife. I was broke, and I was broken.

And I had no idea what to do next.

I'd never experienced such fear in my life. I convinced myself that my destiny had become a trailer park and food stamps.

It wasn't as though I'd never had a job or learned to manage money.

I'd been raised an only child in an upper-middle class household; my parents owned a boat and a second home and belonged to a country club, and they'd always been responsible stewards of their money. They instilled that in me early on. When I was a kid, my mother gave me $1 a week for allowance. I rarely spent it, and there was rarely anything I really wanted to buy. I'd save up $12 or $15 at a time and buy myself something I really wanted, or I'd hang onto it longer.

As a child, I was always looking for ways to make money, always selling things. I'd collect shells on the beach, paint them and sell them as ashtrays.

My first real paychecks started when I was 16, when I declared I needed a car and my father declared I needed a job. My dad agreed to help me buy a car if I could come up with the first $350. So I got a job at a thrift store and worked my way up to manager.

After college, I'd started my own resale shop. I worked hard, poured my heart into it, and I always did well; in fact, I'd made more money than my previous husband with that shop. So I was sitting pretty after I sold it.

And a friend who thought I might have an eye for design hired me to decorate the luxury suites at Veterans Stadium in Philadelphia, home to the Phillies baseball team and the Eagles football team.

I'd had a lot of success early in my life, in fact, but then I packed up and moved from Philadelphia to Los Angeles at age 36, met my dreamy doctor-husband and fell madly and deeply in forever-love. Or so I had thought, when I was seeing the stars and rockets 10 years earlier.

ᘒᘓ ᘒᘓ ᘒᘓ ᘒᘓ ᘒᘓ

I was painfully aware that I had to create a new life for myself. I had to work because I was desperate — financially and emotionally. The modest settlement I received in the divorce was going fast. I was living off my now ex-husband's pension, and then his 401K, but bleeding it dry at a rate of more than $15,000 a month with just the "basics" — the mortgage payment, car and boat payments, and other expenses from our former life together that he simply couldn't be bothered with anymore. The divorce lawyer alone cost me $65,000.

My husband had knocked me on my ass, and I became fragile and broken and scared to death.

I knew I couldn't go back. I couldn't recreate the success I'd had with my thrift shop in my 20s and 30s. I needed my own identity, my own life, and I was determined to make that happen.

I had lost my legs and it was time to get them back.

Chapter 2

The Oddest, Smartest Phone Call I Ever Made

One afternoon in 1993, about a year after my husband left, I sat in the hair dresser's chair at the salon, a black nylon cape around my shoulders, pouring my heart out to my stylist, Dean. I was lamenting to him that I didn't know how many more times I was going to be able to afford his high-priced salon services.

"What am I going to do now? I'm no kid," I said as Dean colored my hair. "I have to get a job. I have to work, and I don't know what to do or where to begin."

The hair dresser at the next chair had overheard my cries of desperation.

"Go to makeup school," he said casually.

"What?" I asked. "What are you talking about?"

I didn't know the first thing about makeup; wasn't even a fan of it. I'd always bypassed glossy tubes of colorful lipstick for Chap Stick or medicated lip balm.

Bobbie Weiner

"Go to makeup school," he said again. "With your personality, you would be great."

I wasn't buying it.

"You want me to learn how to apply makeup on someone like me?" I asked in disbelief, almost humored by the thought of making up customers at the mall. "Work at Saks Fifth Avenue or Macy's and apply makeup to women who live in Beverly Hills?"

He shook his head. "Oh, my God, no!" he said. "Go to learn makeup for the TV and film industry."

"Are you kidding me?" I asked again as I stared at him blankly, still imagining myself spritzing perfume and dabbing blush on the women I'd once played tennis with.

My only real experience with serious makeup application had been much, much earlier in my life. An awkward teenager suffering from very low self-esteem, I'd entered a few Miss America-organized beauty pageants at my mother's unshakably strong urging. I'd gotten my face all made up, put on some pretty clothes, plunked a Barbra Streisand song on the piano, and I'd usually finished as first runner-up, winning a few scholarships here and there. I'd hardly given beauty pageants another thought for 25 years. And now to be a part of the "beauty world?"

"I'm not kidding," the stylist said again.

"Where do you go for this?" I asked, relenting and admittedly curious.

"There are three schools," he explained. "One in Paris, one in Toronto and the Joe Blasco Make-Up School in Hollywood."

I'll never know what made me do it, but I stood up immediately, walked to the pay phone in the back of the salon and called information. I took a breath and dialed the number to the Joe Blasco Makeup School.

ОЮ ОЮ ОЮ ОЮ ОЮ

The very next day, I sat nervously in front of the director and the head makeup teacher. After I told them my story, they handed me a piece of paper with an outline of a face and a pencil. They asked me to fill in the face and shade it. I did as they asked, and two weeks later, I was a student in makeup school.

The weekend before classes started, I met my friend Mary for lunch. We'd played tennis for years at the Riviera Country Club, back when we both were living picture-perfect, Technicolor-fairy tale existences. The veteran of a bitter divorce herself, Mary was a psychologist who raised her son alone. So when I voiced my second thoughts about going to makeup school, I trusted whatever she might advise.

"Go to school!" Mary exclaimed. "Do it and don't look back! This is a great opportunity. Go for it!"

I respected Mary's level-headed answer, and I needed that extra shove she gave me.

The next morning, I surveyed the room of 14 students in the classroom. I looked like everyone's mother.

It would be OK, I reminded myself. I was there to learn a trade, to get a profession; I needed to make money doing something. It was either this or working at Gap, I thought. I tried to imagine myself folding sweaters for a living and couldn't quite get my brain to go there. I was 46 years old, and it was time to move past what had happened to me, into what could happen next.

My dad often said, "Bobs, you get one ticket when you come into this life and you have choices."

So I was making my choice now, deciding that no matter what it took, I was going to be a makeup artist for TV and film.

ೞ ೞ ೞ ೞ ೞ

In the beginning, I was a little heavy handed with the makeup. But no other student — not one of those 20- or 30-somethings — tried harder than the "old lady" of the class. I stayed after school for two hours every day watching how-to videos in a small room by myself. I studied the tapes renowned artist Joe Blasco had made of his own work, determined to master this new craft.

The school constantly fielded calls for makeup artists — for fashion shows and charity luncheons and film schools requesting a makeup artist for a student's thesis or music video. As soon as the calls came in, our director would pop into the classroom and ask who wanted work that weekend. I was always the first to raise my hand.

These jobs paid maybe $25 for gas money or a kit fee if you used your own makeup. But I had nothing better to do on weekends; the work filled my hours and provided me with valuable practice. I embraced every opportunity for experience as a makeup artist like a weekend warrior. My glory days on the Riviera tennis court were over.

Truthfully, I could afford to work for almost nothing because I still had some of my husband's 401K money left. I knew I would need these experiences and felt fortunate that my entire livelihood didn't depend on them.

One of my very first jobs, which I did for free, was for a USC film student's thesis project. This kid was the son of a notable Hollywood director who'd given him $100,000 to produce this little film (I never asked which one, and to this day I don't know ... I didn't want to jeopardize the job by asking something nosy like that). It was being shot at some flop-house motel in downtown L.A., and when I pulled up in my Jeep, I became overwhelmed with emotion. With the electrical equipment and the actors and the costumers (who'd run to Nordstrom and buy clothes on the Hollywood-dad's credit card), it looked like a real set.

"I hope you know what you're doing," someone said to me when I walked in. One of the tasks was to make an actor look dirty, and the head makeup artist had sent someone to McDonald's to get mustard and ketchup and other condiments to use as dirty makeup. It smelled like garbage, but I got such a rush from being around it.

ดจ ดจ ดจ ดจ ดจ

In class, every face I made up looked like Tammy Faye Bakker's: WAY overdone. Everyone says makeup should enhance natural beauty; my heavy hand made the models look anything but natural.

But my tendency to overdo it was actually going to pay off.

"Learn how to do everything," I remembered that hairstylist who'd first encouraged me to go to makeup school saying. "Everyone wants to make actors and models look pretty. You'll be much more valuable if you can make them look ugly, too. If they're going to take you out of the country on location, they'll want you to do more than just beauty makeup."

I found myself — and my heavy hand — gravitating toward special effects makeup. Most people make it through the first few weeks and stop because they've learned how to make people look good. I stayed on — what else did I have to do? They would regularly bring in "old timers" to teach special techniques, such as the makeup artist from Cone Heads, who taught me how to do bald cap and cone head looks.

They really worked with me, and we would laugh and joke at how heavy handed I was. When they were teaching old age, I didn't make my models look like they'd aged; I made them look like disgusting monsters.

I was practicing my bruises, burns and broken bones more than anyone else in the class.

Practice paid off. As one of the final tests to graduate from Joe Blasco, we had to simulate first, second and third-degree burns on a model, beard them, put bullet holes in their face and break their nose. When my model, my new hairstylist I'd convinced to sit for me, took one look at his mangled body in a mirror, he threw up all over himself right before the teacher graded me.

"I guess you have your answer," the teacher, Mr. Bailey, said when he surveyed my work and the fresh vomit covering my model. "This is the best work I have ever seen; the most amazing burns and bullet holes."

It was one of the highest compliments I'd ever received. Now, after the three months of required training at the Joe Blasco school, I was hungry for opportunities to stretch and grow.

"I can do this; I know I can," I kept telling myself as I transitioned into the high-pressure real world of TV and film.

Chapter 3

Bloody Mary Is Born

Three days after graduation, Mr. Bailey called me.

"They are shooting a horror film in the valley at the Gene Barry Ranch, and the makeup department needs another pair of hands," he said. "They are paying $35.00 for 12-plus hours. This is a great opportunity, Bobbie, and you will get to learn production etiquette and be on a real movie set. It is a low budget horror film, Pumpkinhead II."

Little did I know, he already had been turned down by two other students in my class who refused to work for such little pay on a low-budget movie. I wasn't going to let the opportunity pass.

"Where do I go and what time?" I asked.

"Just show up and don't bring anything," he advised. "You will probably be a gofer for the key makeup artist and her assistant."

I had to be there at 5 p.m. — in about two hours — so I pulled on my jeans and ran out the door. I looked at my makeup kit but left it behind as he had instructed me. Instead, I stuffed a carton of cigarettes into my backpack. I didn't smoke, but Mr. Bailey had advised me to always carry a carton of cigarettes on assignments.

"When you are on set," he had explained, "you make sure you have a carton at all times, because at 3 in the morning when the crew runs out of smokes, you break out your cigarettes. No one will ever forget the makeup artist with the cigarettes." This proved to be one of the smartest things I learned from Mr. Bailey.

At the ranch, a van was waiting for me at the bottom of the hill. I parked my Jeep, jumped into the van and stepped into my new life. The driver climbed up the hill into the mountains of the Santa Clarita Valley, and I was now a crew member of Pumpkinhead II. Inside the makeup trailer, the key makeup artist put me to work immediately. The trailer was full of actors and stunt people, and the entire area was buzzing with excitement.

The key makeup artist threw a box of Kleenex into my hands and sent me off to the set with an actress. We waited for lighting to finish and when the actress stepped into the scene, I blotted and wiped the sweat from her face. This was the best — a real job! I would have paid them for the opportunity.

After they finished the shot, we returned to the trailer, where I was immediately tasked with applying makeup to actors. I hesitated when I came to a beautiful black actress, confessing to her that I didn't have experience applying makeup to black skin. She had brought her own supplies.

"Honey," she said, "I'm gonna teach you how to do black makeup." And she did, providing me with yet another invaluable lesson on this $35-job.

After I worked on a string of actors, the key makeup artist approached and said, "They need me to dress the dollhouse with blood. Will you do it?"

"Sure!" I said, throwing myself into yet another blind situation.

She loaded my hands with a small bottle of stage blood, a handful of Q-tips and small brushes. The production assistant led me into an old

14

barn, to a dollhouse, an exact replica of the set. I dressed the dollhouse with blood — placing it on the little dolls, the furniture, walls and carpeting — to prepare it to be blown up. When I looked up from my designer bloodbath, about 20 people were watching me, engrossed in what I was doing. They were like a hungry family hovering over the cook in the kitchen, and I couldn't believe I was the cook.

In that moment I became an important part of the crew. No one was rushing me, and despite all the eyes being on my work in a hushed atmosphere, I did not feel nervous. I emerged from my assignment covered with blood on my face, arms and legs. I was a sticky mess, but I knew I had done something worthwhile. I hadn't felt this important in a long, long time; my ex-husband had taken away most of my self-worth, and I needed this moment.

Nothing could ever beat this, I thought as I cleaned myself up. But something was about to.

The key makeup artist asked me to go on the closed set with two actors. I had no idea what a "closed set" meant, but so far I was doing pretty well with these ventures into the unknown.

She handed me another box of Kleenex and sent me off with another production assistant. As we approached the set, we saw fire trucks, fire marshals and paramedics assembled outside the room where we were to shoot the scene.

When we got closer, someone yelled, "Here comes Bloody Mary," and the crew clapped and cheered. They had named me Bloody Mary, I found out, after my work on the dollhouse. That night "Bloody Mary" was born.

I had achieved a new identity, and this was it, I realized just then. The Doctor's Wife was long gone.

When we got to the set, I discovered that "closed" meant someone was half-naked. They strapped a gas mask on my face and I stepped onto the set, geared up for a lot of smoke and fog. Later I learned that a monster, "Pumpkinhead," was going to rise from the ground to attack people.

After the scene wrapped, we broke for dinner at 11 p.m. Just six hours after I had arrived, I'd become part of the crew family. I was flying high. After dinner, we all went back to work, and now I was making up stunt doubles — some of the most important people on these types of action films. No sooner did I transform one into an old lady then the next "victim" would enter the trailer. This went on until the wee hours, about 3 a.m., when I brought out the gold — the cigarettes.

By 6 a.m. it was time to go home. A producer's assistant asked me to step into an office on the set where — I couldn't believe my luck — they invited me to finish up the film for them. They offered me $100 for three weeks of work. I had a paying job, and I couldn't have been prouder of that $100 opportunity.

After that night, the word spread: "Bloody Mary" was a keeper.

ⓧ ⓧ ⓧ ⓧ ⓧ

I became the new assistant to the key makeup artist. I finished my three weeks and as soon as the shoot ended, I was offered another movie assignment. They were lining up crew and would start shooting in a few months. (At last – something to look forward to!) Pumpkinhead II wrapped on a Saturday, I partied with the crew on Sunday, and two days later I received another call from the makeup school.

When I answered the phone, Tate Holland, the school's director, was on the other line.

"Bobbie, what are you doing?" he asked. And before I could answer, he exclaimed, "They need a makeup artist over at HBO Studios in Hollywood. Now! The makeup artist did not show up …"

Before he could finish, I was asking for the address of the studio. All I could think about was getting an HBO credit on my resume. Twenty minutes later, I walked into a roomful of actors happy to see me. I set to work immediately, unaware that the public relations agent in charge of this new movie had just started work a few months earlier, landing this film as his agency's first big job.

The actors were delighted with the makeup I'd applied, especially Katherine Helmond (known for her roles in Who's the Boss? and Soap), She was an older actress who quickly came to trust me — an older-than-average makeup artist. Helmond and the other actors asked what I was doing the following evening. They were to promote this film on Entertainment Tonight, she said, and they needed a makeup artist. This would be perfect, I thought — HBO and ET in two days' time. I felt very, very lucky.

As I packed my kit, the president of the PR agency asked what he owed me.

"Nothing," I said. "Don't worry about it. I'll see you tomorrow night."

"You saved my life," he replied emphatically.

But the PR agent had no idea that he was saving my life. The following night, I arrived at the studio 45 minutes early and met the Entertainment Tonight crew. I sat with them and waited for the stars to show up. They were impressed that I was already set up and ready to apply makeup upon their arrival. The president of the agency gave me a big hug. I completed their hair and makeup and stayed until the last shoot to make sure everyone looked great for the cameras. As I was leaving, the owner of the agency once again asked me how much he owed me.

"My pleasure!" I blurted out.

Incredulous, he looked at me and said, "I owe you. I will never forget what you did for me."

Six months later, those same Entertainment Tonight producers decided to do a segment on makeovers. Remembering how much they had enjoyed my professionalism and friendliness, they invited me to feature my work on the show. We shot at the Joe Blasco School, and I brought my own model — an 83-year-old actress with whom I'd worked on a short film and who often appeared in commercials. When we walked in, people were shocked that I'd brought such an old model. But my philosophy was: why demonstrate on a hot, young model if I was supposed to show off a dramatic makeover? My "before and after" transformation impressed them; I'd made the model appear about 20 years younger.

ৰ৵ ৰ৵ ৰ৵ ৰ৵ ৰ৵

After that, the jobs kept rolling in. Within six weeks of Pumpkinhead II, I'd started making $1,200 a week. My teacher told me to charge $300 a day; I got $400 a day for commercials. I also developed a rapport with older actresses because they thought I did a better job with their makeup than younger makeup artists did, so they regularly hired me.

So, there I was. I had a career. I had gotten my foot in the door and then blown it wide open. In a short time, I proved to be a team player — a punctual, reliable, well-prepared artist who was happy to be working and easy to get along with. Those qualities ensure that you are remembered by everyone after the job is done.

No one forgot me or the cigarettes I brought on that very first professional job —especially not with a name like Bloody Mary.

I had to make another interesting and unexpected change around about this time: my name. My first name was really Barbara, and I'd always gone by the nickname Bobby. One day a good friend of mine — a guy who went to my gym and happened to be Sylvester Stallone's bodyguard — told me I was making a big mistake by going by "Bobby."

"What do you mean a mistake?" I thought. "That's my name."

He told me to change the spelling from "Bobby" to "Bobbie" so people would know right away I was female. See, in the early- to mid-1990s, when AIDS was making headlines and raising a lot of fears, people in Hollywood were reluctant to hire male makeup artists. They were afraid of getting AIDS through close contact with those were infected. Sometimes guys were showing up on the sets with Band-Aids on their neck and hands, and they were covering their sores. To be safe, many production companies would hire only female makeup artists.

My friend thought I would get more makeup jobs if people knew right away they'd be hiring a female. The unfortunate truth is: he was right.

Chapter 4

Working for a Living

After Pumpkinhead II, I routinely got called to do short films and B-list horror movies (most of the names aren't even worth mentioning because they went straight to video; you won't find them on the Internet Movie Database, even.) Although I wasn't living a luxurious lifestyle as I once had, I was bringing in paychecks of $900 to $1,200 per week when I was working — which was regulary. I enjoyed meeting interesting people and traveling around the country. My life felt more fulfilled than it had in a long time.

For the first time since my divorce, I started to bond with people — people whom I could call true friends. (God knows I lost all of my Bel Air buddies when the money went away.)

One of the most influential people I met at this time in my life (and, to this day, one of the most special people who has ever entered my life) was a young woman named Kimber. She was about 24 years old and from Philadelphia, just like I was. I met her while we both were working a documentary for a lawyer. We became fast friends; she had the best sense of humor and we shared a lot of laughs, on set and off. She and I loved working together.

Kimber was so creative — she could make a wedding gown out of a napkin. Soon we worked together on a horror film, and then we both got hired to work on a cheesy soft porn film.

One day on set, Kimber complained that her foot had fallen asleep and that she was having trouble moving it. The next day, the feeling moved up her leg. She was admitted to the hospital, and I hardly left her side.

Five weeks later, she died of a brain tumor. Kimber's sudden and tragic death shook me up like nothing I'd experienced since my divorce. She was so young, so beautiful and so talented. I couldn't believe my dear friend's life had been cut so short.

To this day, I still think about Kimber. Her tragic story influenced my life; she's one reason I always think about taking the bull by the horns, grabbing opportunities and living life to the fullest. You'd better live your life and enjoy it, I often think, because you never know when it might all come to an end.

ᘓᘔ ᘓᘔ ᘓᘔ ᘓᘔ ᘓᘔ

Film after film, job after job, one of the best — and worst — things about being a Hollywood makeup artist was traveling to new sets on new locations. You dropped into a new place, do your job, enjoy your surroundings and then leave to go back home. But there could be unexpected complications in these new locations — little snags you weren't used to — such as the weather.

In 1995, I was elated to get a film job in South Florida. I arrived in Miami Beach on May 20, but shooting got delayed because of terrifying thunderstorms. (Much of the shoot was to be on the water — and water, plus boats, plus lightning, equal a risky combination.) While I was there,

I got a call from a New York production company to work on a film they were shooting in Miami. I signed on right away, which made my parents very happy, as they lived in Miami.

The wretched, rainy weather and brutal lightning dragged on, and I grew bored out of my mind. On July 19, I got two memorable telephone calls. The thunder and lightning were so bad that we'd been advised not to turn on the TV or talk on the phone. But when my pager went off and I saw the California area code, I called back anyway.

When I found out who the first call came from, I felt like I'd been struck by a thunderbolt myself. It was the office of legendary TV writer-producer Steven Bochco, the man behind Hill Street Blues, L.A. Law and later, NYPD Blue. I could hardly believe Stephen Bochco was calling me!

He was looking for a makeup artist for his new show Murder One. I was ready to jump on a plane and fly back to California to get Steven Bochco on my resume, but there was one problem: I wasn't union. He needed a unionized makeup artist, and I hadn't worked enough to be union yet. Reluctantly, I had to pass up that opportunity.

But then the phone rang again. It was 1:30 in the morning, still storming outside. The second caller was the producer of a TV show in San Diego.

"Are you Bobbie Weiner?" the gentleman on the other end asked.

"Yes," I replied.

"I heard you are just the old lady makeup artist I need to straighten out my makeup trailer," he said.

"Calling me 'old lady' will cost you," I joked.

The name of the show was Renegade, he said. It starred the long-haired, well-chiseled heartthrob Lorenzo Lamas. They had been through a few different makeup artists, he explained, but these "young things" were having a bit of a problem with schoolgirl crushes on Lorenzo. He didn't just need a good makeup artist; he needed someone he could trust not to develop any romantic notions about the star. ("Old lady" to the rescue, indeed!)

ᘉ ᘉ ᘉ ᘉ ᘉ

Two days later, I was on my way to meet the actors and producers of my first TV show. I passed with flying colors at our first meeting. I signed the usual eight-month contract (with four months of hiatus between seasons). And when I met the hairdresser who would share the trailer with me — a fellow Virgo named Julie (who happened to be the producer's wife), who shared my birthday – we hit it off like old friends. Another young lady, Josie, who was from England, interned as a makeup artist on the set. We also became fast friends, but she quickly decided she liked hair much better and returned home to England to pursue her career. Little did I know at the time that Josie would soon lead me to the single biggest career move of my life.

I became Lorenzo Lamas' personal makeup artist on Renegade and worked on the other actors too, including Stephen Cannell. Cannell is one of the only Hollywood stars I can honestly say I was friends with. He was the rare star who made friends with the "help," even occasionally helping me to carry my makeup and supplies to the car after a long day. He died in 2010, and the world lost a great, great guy.

I wasn't just any makeup artist or crew member on the Renegade set. I was the old woman, the "momma" whom the producers and directors would count on to help the actors start shooting with their heads on straight, so to speak. For this, I earned the respect of the actors and producers alike. Eight great months of full-time work and then it was hiatus time.

ᘉ ᘉ ᘉ ᘉ ᘉ

During hiatus, I kept busy with movies of the week, and squeezed in some Showtime gigs. I also got a taste, for the first time, of what entrepreneurial success might feel like – and of how risky it might be.

One day at the La Jolla post office, as I was putting pictures of some of the Renegade stars into big envelopes, the woman next to me asked how I knew them.

"I do their makeup on the TV show," I said.

This woman was a star-chaser (or, to use a less flattering but well-known term in Southern California, a "star-f***er.") She liked the show and wanted to be my buddy right way. We became friends, and I started playing tennis with her husband. At the time, I didn't know anyone except for crew from the show, and I was single and dateless, so I enjoyed the company of friends.

This woman's husband, who was in marketing and was always thinking up new ideas, had some entrepreneurial juices flowing; he wanted to use my talent, knowledge and creativity to come up with some new products. He was a book broker for Crown Books, and one day he approached me about making some children's projects that would be connected to books so they could be sold in bookstores.

I said sure — why not? I was on hiatus and didn't have much else going on. All I had to do was write a little book and attach a little kids' project to it. I'd never done something like this and didn't have young kids of my own, so I began my research at the best place I could think of — the mall. I visited a nature store and found some interesting things that sparked ideas for books that I thought kids might like.

Within a week, I was writing a book for children on butterfly gardens — complete with information on how to get their own silkworms and create their own butterfly garden. I did another one on volcanoes and turned it into an at-home volcano kit. I also created my first face paint kits for children. Working without a computer, I started to amass a leather-bound organizer full of contacts and resources for these projects

— dozens of names and phone numbers scribbled on bits of paper that, to this day, still stuff the notebook full.

The man went nuts for my creations; he flew me to Bakersfield to meet with a butterfly farm about supplying real butterflies to promote the butterfly garden project. They loved them, too. I got myself an artist, and the books and makeup kits went to production.

During this whole process, he paid me $300 a week. But I didn't care at first — I was having fun! I was dumb as mud.

Pretty soon, they were flying me to Butterfly World in Florida to get butterflies for a booth at a book convention in Chicago. For our booth, I'd recreated the butterfly garden, complete with real butterflies. I also was painting kids' faces and promoting my kits, which said "created by a Hollywood Makeup Artist." The business at the Chicago fair was insane; you couldn't get near our booth.

The man I was working for came by our booth with some very important-looking businessmen, and I found it odd that he never introduced me to them. The line for our booth was out the door, and here I was the creator of these popular products, and he didn't give me the time of day. He treated me like I was his salesgirl, not the brains behind the whole operation. Something was fishy.

A guy from Barnes & Noble, on the other hand, couldn't get enough of me and my products. He and his three adorable kids hung around the booth for a long time, while I painted the kids' faces and talked about the books. The face paint kits said nothing more than, "created by a Hollywood makeup artist." This guy saw the potential right away.

"I've got to thank you," the man said. "...what you're doing for my kids, I should pay you."

He handed me his card and said, "Do me a favor. When your name is on something, you call me."

When I returned to my boss' office in La Jolla, the people from

Renegade called. It was time to go back to my real job. But I wanted to wrap up this project, too.

"How'd you do?" I asked my boss excitedly after what I was sure was a home-run at the book convention.

"Not that well," he replied. I was shocked. Not that well? We had kids climbing on each other to get to the butterfly garden, and we did "not that well?"

I knew right then that he was lying to me, and then I found proof. I walked past the fax machine, where the orders came spewing in, one after another. Wal-mart alone ordered about 92,000 of MY face paint kits.

For $300 a week, I had created a business for this guy — a mini empire, even, and he was going to leave me high and dry. I'd had enough of the whole thing. He could make 92,000 face paint kits by himself.

"I'm going back to Renegade," I told him on a Friday afternoon and packed up my stuff to leave.

"You can't," he replied tersely. "I need you here Monday morning."

"What do you mean you NEED me here?" I asked. "I'm not going to be here."

He said he needed me there to talk to some higher-ups at the company about the products. I was the only one who really knew about them and could present them to these guys. "These guys," it turned out, were from North Carolina. My "boss" was their director of marketing and product development, and he was being paid upwards of $150,000 to come up with new products. I created the products and he turned around and sold them; $150,000 for him and $300 a week for me. What a jackass.

That guy had a gold mine with me and he blew it.

I called my father. He was outraged. By Saturday morning, he'd hired a lawyer and an accountant. I met with them that afternoon. They told me I had to detach myself from this horrible man immediately. We set up a meeting with the guy for Sunday afternoon.

And while my boss shook hands and said hello to my lawyer and accountant, he couldn't even look at me. They told me to keep my mouth shut. The lawyer and accountant walked into my boss' conference room, which he'd turned into a showroom filled with my impressive products. The short meeting went something like this:

Lawyer to my boss: "You've got some pretty fabulous things here. Who created these?"

My boss: "Bobbie did. I have to have her here tomorrow morning. The people coming from North Carolina will be here, and they own everything. I need her. I need her."

Lawyer: "Wow, you paid her $300 a week to make all this stuff and you need her so badly? What do you think she's really worth?"

My boss: "Probably about the same as a stay-at-home mom is worth. About $17,500."

Lawyer: "OK, well Bobbie is not going to work for $17,500, and Bobbie is going to gather her things, and we're going to walk out of here."

The guy turned sheet-white. The lawyer and accountant waited for me, I got my organizer and the picture of my dead dog on my desk, and gave him back my key. That night I flew to Florida to be with my parents. I had to be away from the whole mess.

I'd actually gotten tickets for the guy's wife and me to attend Bill Maher's show in La Jolla the next weekend, and she had the nerve to call and ask if we were still going.

"Absolutely not," I said. And when I hung up, I never spoke to or saw either of them again.

Later, after I went into business for myself, the guys from North Carolina came after me. After all, they had been paying for everything while I worked for this guy, including some "perks" my boss was taking from them, like a lavish ski vacation that the couple took me along on. If he took me, of course, the vacation could be a "business expense" and he could charge the company for the whole thing. And he did. My lawyer defended me, and I didn't have to pay a dime.

The guy got canned from that company. He went bankrupt. The couple divorced.

I rarely talk about this part of my life because it was really hurtful. What this whole painful ordeal taught me, though, was that I had the ability to make something out of nothing, and to be really sucessful at it! Remembering what the Barnes & Noble guy had said to me at the book convention in Florida, my entrepreneurial spirit was awakened. And never again did I made anything that I didn't put my own name on — and get it trademarked.

Little did I know, bigger things were headed my way next. Much, much bigger.

Chapter 5

The Titanic Sinks and My Career Rises

Just as we were about to return to work on Renegade, in 1996, I got a call from England. It came from the key makeup artist for a film on location in Mexico, who'd gotten my name and a glowing recommendation from Josie, the former Renegade intern. This little film was called Titanic with James Cameron as director and producer. I had heard of this film — who hadn't? — especially in the film industry. Production was scheduled to start in one month.

They'd heard about my work as a makeup artist on horror films, about how "Bloody Mary" could transform mild-mannered people into grotesque monsters. They needed my special effects skills to help create the ice-blue, stone-cold, floating corpses of Titanic passengers.

The significance of this project shocked and excited me. I knew I could do what they were asking, and a James Cameron credit on my resume would be huge, yet I initially turned it down and then asked for more time to make my decision. The film was shooting in Rosarita, Mexico, near Tijuana — not the safest nor the most desirable place for a single, middle-aged woman to live, even for a short time. I did speak Spanish, but reports of violence and thefts near the set still frightened me; my father advised me not to go. Besides, Renegade would be starting again soon, and I'd have to abandon it to work on Titanic.

"Let me think about it," I told the makeup artist.

Two weeks later she called back, saying they were in Mexico and asked me to drive down. Hesitantly, I agreed, and a few days later I was south of the border. When a group of people in the makeup department asked what I could do to make someone look dead and frozen, I demonstrated my technique. I learned, to my surprise, that they were timing me. I was making them look stone cold in 7 minutes flat. They were impressed. And persuasive.

This WOULD be a great opportunity, I decided — Titanic and James Cameron on my resume would be pure gold. We negotiated the salary, and the money they were willing to pay me was incredible — after all, I argued, I'd have to give up my steady-paying job on Renegade to work on this project. I started working on Titanic a week later. For 18 hours a day, 6 days a week, 5 weeks straight, I painted blue lips and icicles on people.

I never moved to Mexico for the shoot. Each day I awoke at 4 a.m. and made the two-hour drive from my home in La Jolla, outside San Diego. The border guards got to know me well. Someone suggested I slip them a 20-dollar bill to slide into Mexico faster, without a search. No way I was doing that; what did I have to hide? Every day, coming and going, my car (which had a Titanic crew sticker on the window) got stopped and searched.

Each night, I would drive back to La Jolla and sleep in my own bed. I knew precisely the point on the road, past the border, at which I could pop in a Tylenol PM, be alert enough to drive the rest of the way but fall asleep as soon as my head hit the pillow.

The challenge of working on the Titanic set provided an adrenaline rush every day. I made up to 35 actors each day. I had a powerful incentive to do well. Cameron threatened to throw me in "the tank" – a huge hot tub made to look like the frozen ocean — if the actors' makeup came off or needed significant touch-ups. The tank was disgusting — 75 people, wearing multiple layers of clothing, in one hot tub for 4 or 5 hours at one time; you can imagine how gross it got each day.

I wasn't going anywhere near that toilet bowl.

To make sure of it, I added my own ingredients to the makeup the studio provided and made sure it was water-resistant and sweat-proof; I tripled-layered the setting powder on each one. I am proud to say I never got thrown in the tank to reapply makeup.

The set of Titanic was famously secretive. Anyone who worked on it had to sign a strict contract — no drinking, no drug use, and absolutely NO talking about the film off-set.

It took 5 weeks to complete my initial assignment — the dead people in the ocean. Then they needed help with some other scenes with a lot of actors, such as the "steerage party" scene — the one in which Leonardo DiCaprio and Kate Winslet's characters dance and drink below deck with the commoners. The money was great, so I ended up staying on for a few more days. And then I was done…but not before I'd have another odd twist of fate that would lead me headfirst into establishing my own business.

കൗ കൗ കൗ കൗ കൗ

On a Sunday morning at 5 a.m., our only day off from the Titanic shoot, one of Leonardo DiCaprio's stunt doubles asked me for blue and gold makeup. He and a few friends were going to a San Diego Chargers game and wanted to paint their faces in honor of the team, he said. I gave him a bag of makeup and some sponges and off he went. The next morning when he came into makeup, I asked, "How was the game?"

To my surprise, he didn't give me any feedback on the game — just on the makeup. He raved about it, saying, "We were on TV and everyone wanted to know where we got the face paint."

"You're kidding," I said. "What did you use before?"

When he told me Magic markers and Sharpies, all I could think was, "Oh boy!"

The creative wheels in my head started turning.

I finished my work on Titanic and went back to San Diego, ready to return to Los Angeles. I didn't want to go back to Renegade; I'd decided I wanted to take a stab at developing some sports makeup. Before I left San Diego for L.A., I grabbed a good-looking 26-year-old guy working at a coffee shop in La Jolla that I frequented. I asked him a random question: "Could I paint your face?"

I painted his face using the same colors, blue and gold, just like I gave to the stunt double for the Chargers game. I took some photos and used his face on a mock-up kit with blue and gold face paint. I wanted to come up with durable, convenient makeup that sports fans could apply easily on the fly, without water or sponges. I drove to Los Angeles and walked into UCLA on a Tuesday morning, asking for the buyer of accessories. What a huge score! It was like entering a gigantic department store. I showed the salesclerk my kit; he thought it was great and directed me upstairs to the buyers' offices. I had no appointment and no idea what I was doing, but I needed to show this idea and show it fast.

Upstairs, I asked another salesman where I could meet the buyer and a few minutes later a nice man came out to meet me. I presented my face paint kit; he took me to his office and told me it was a great concept. (I had no idea the Bruins' school colors were blue and gold, a fortunate twist of fate.) The buyer said he had never seen anything like my kit, and told me I had to attend something called CAMEX, a college trade show that was coming up in three weeks in Las Vegas.

Once again, I jumped at the opportunity. "What do I do and whom do I call?"

He picked up the phone and made the connection for me. Within 20 minutes I reserved a booth for $1,200 and was making plans to go to Las Vegas. I drove back to San Diego and called my model, Seth, to enlist his help. He agreed to take off work and got his young wife's permission to attend the Las Vegas convention with me. Two weeks later we landed in Vegas.

೧೦ ೧೦ ೧೦ ೧೦ ೧೦

On the first night, Seth and I went to the meet-and-greet cocktail party. I brought a backpack full of Sports Fan Face Paints business cards — hot off the press. The room was packed. Over 1,000 people and in the center of it all stood a huge 20 foot table, where waiters and waitresses were serving free beer, wine and soft drinks to everyone. Tables were set up throughout that enormous conference room and the servers were clearly short-handed, so I said to Seth, "Get your 'tookis' over there and ask if you can help."

I gave him two handfuls of my business cards and told him to hand them all out. With his face still painted in bold colors, Seth was soon behind the table helping the hotel staff. The cocktail reception lasted an hour and Seth passed out many more cards from my backpack, smiling away in his face paint like a fan in search of a football game.

Throughout the convention, Seth was a walking billboard. He sported my face paint for the entire three days and nights, working the crowd as my right hand. We were treated like rock stars, and I knew in my gut I was on to something hot that had never been done.

The woman in the adjoining booth could not believe the action in my little 10-by-10 booth. On the second day I went to her booth, briefly told her my background and story and she said, "Just take orders! Get business cards and we'll have dinner tonight and talk."

Regina sold big rain ponchos in school colors. She had been making the circuit for years and she was terrific. Everyone knew her and spoke kindly of her. Regina turned out to be a huge help, guiding me in the right direction. She advised me on what to sell and how to price the paints — I didn't even know what to charge.

Armed only with business cards and Seth's colorful face, goodwill and hutzpah, we left our first convention with 46 orders for face paint kits. We sold to the country's leading universities, as well as a few small colleges, and a major distributor signed me up. My spirits were soaring … I was on my way to owning and operating a makeup company.

Now I just had to figure out how the hell to do that.

ᘒᘔ ᘒᘔ ᘒᘔ ᘒᘔ ᘒᘔ

Before I'd taken the Titanic job, I'd fully intended to come back to television work when it was over. But now my life had taken a different turn, and I was getting a business off the ground.

I decided that in the year before the movie came out, I'd take the money I made from it and try to develop my own company. It took a lot of money, for a lot of things that people might not think about. For one thing, I had to pay my makeup manufacturers up front. I had to buy the packaging (called "blister cards") and hire an artist to design them.

I was putting all I had into this new business — literally, all my time and money. To help cover my own living expenses, I sold my car. Without a home of my own — or even an apartment to rent (who could afford that?) — I rented a bedroom in different people's houses. I ended up having to do that for five years.

I started my little business in the garage of a condo where I rented a room. I didn't care that I didn't have a "real" office yet. I had a feeling I was onto something — something that was my own, and I was already feeling proud.

I had another secret weapon in my back pocket — James Cameron on my resume. The sinking of the Titanic on the big screen was about to lead to the rise of my company.

Working on Titanic was the best marketing tool I could have imagined.

I had been one of the first crew to leave the set, and when I came back, I called and wrote to every local news organization I could think of to get my name and my Titanic association. People were thrilled with anticipation for this movie, and although I couldn't divulge any secrets, I sure could show anyone who'd watch how I made up the dead, frozen actors.

ᘓᘐ ᘓᘐ ᘓᘐ ᘓᘐ ᘓᘐ

Before Titanic came out, someone suggested I contact The Learning Annex in San Diego, an institute where people took professional and personal development seminars. I wanted to learn how to become a public speaker and do seminars, and that's a course they were offering. As soon as the marketing director giving the class found out I was interested in conducting a course called "Secrets of a Hollywood Makeup Artist," she thought I was a goldmine. She made me the guinea pig of the class. I did a proposal to the Learning Annex. Next thing I knew, they signed me up for a few sessions on how to make women look 5 to 7 years younger, and they brought in a packed house. The women were being charged $35 per class, and when a friend pointed out I was only keeping about $7 per class, he suggested I conduct my own seminars.

So I found space at a local hotel, put a free ad in the paper, charged a lower rate of $30 per person, and filled the seats to capacity. I was giving them tips on how to look younger, like they had gotten a good night's sleep, and I realized I should be selling makeup, too. I got a contractor to mix up some samples, I perfected it, and I sold them age-perfecting makeup under the name "Secrets of a Hollywood Makeup Artist," then TOM – "The Other Makeup." Years later, I made it heavier, and it became The Final Touch, my funeral line.

ৎ৩ ৎ৩ ৎ৩ ৎ৩ ৎ৩

I was still getting calls for makeup jobs, which was great because I didn't have any steady jobs at this point to bring in money while I tried to get my business off the ground. One of the coolest calls I got was from the World Championship Wrestling (WCW) federation. TV wrestling audiences were huge in the '90s, and of course, the guys (and a few women, too) needed someone to paint up their faces before they jumped into the ring to bash each other's brains out. That was a fun gig, the wrestlers were great guys, and everyone whom I worked with at WCW really liked me. In fact, they wanted me to go on the road with them.

But I was focused on my business. This wouldn't be the end of my relationship with the wrestlers, however. A few years later, we'd meet up again and they would be helping ME out a lot.

Chapter 6

New Marching Orders

Another fortuitous media booking I got, a year before Titanic came out, was to appear on a morning TV show in San Diego. They asked me to make up the news anchors like the dead, frozen characters I had created for the Titantic. Of course I said, "Sure!"

They interviewed me, and in between commercials I applied make-up to a couple of the news anchors. At the same time on that early Wednesday morning, someone from the Camp Pendleton Marine base was enjoying his coffee and watching Sun Up San Diego. His attention was sparked when I explained how my Titanic actors' make-up never washed off, even as they lay in the water up to five hours at a time.

He got through to the TV station and asked that I call him when I got off the air. Turned out he was manager of the Camp Pendleton Post Exchange (PX), the base super store for Marines and their families. The next morning I was sitting around a table with him and his staff; he supervised all of the buyers and they all wanted to meet me.

The question of the hour was, "What can you do for us?"

"What do you need?" I asked.

He said simply, "We need a new camouflage make-up."

"What is wrong with the one you use now?" I probed.

They all said the Marines hated it and wouldn't wear it because it made them break out in pimples. It was too greasy or hard as a rock; soldiers had to light matches to soften it. Their wives complained that it stained their collars and clothes and would not wash out. The makeup sticks were hard and would cut their skin when they would apply it.

Their dilemma was clear and the need for something better was obvious.

Once again, I said "yes" and resolved to figure out how to do it.

"You have a deal," they said. They also asked me to paint Marines' children's faces at the opening of a new Toyland store for Halloween.

"You have a deal and you can count on it," I assured them.

ഇ൪ ഇ൪ ഇ൪ ഇ൪ ഇ൪

Driving off the base that Thursday morning, I was already thinking about how I would create a better camouflage paint for them. I took a deep breath, determined to come up with something. Unable to stop the whirlwind in my brain, I changed my clothes to join a friend for coffee that afternoon at the Del Mar beach. We met at 4 p.m. and my pager went off at 4:20. I looked down at an unfamiliar telephone number in San Diego, returned the call and heard a man's voice at the other end.

He jumped right into the subject at hand.

"I just got off the phone with the manager at Camp Pendleton, and I heard you are developing a new camouflage face paint for them. We would like to meet with you."

This gentleman was the head of recruitment at the huge Marine base in San Diego.

At 11 a.m. the following day, I drove down to San Diego's Old

Town district to meet with him and the buyers for the Marine Corps Recruit Depot (MCRD). Our conversation was an instant replay of the one at Camp Pendleton the previous day. They needed a new camo face paint. The guys would not wear what they were selling and issuing to Marine graduates.

In fact, they told me if I succeeded at creating a great new camouflage, the entire United States Military might be interested. They were using a formula from 1918!

This had the potential to be huge for me. I wasn't about to get it wrong.

I looked them straight in the face and made my commitment: "I can do this."

After shaking their hands, I got in my car and called my dad.

"Dad, I think I have something really big going on here," I said excitedly.

"What is going on, Bobs?" he asked.

I explained what had happened in the last two days, the TV show and my meetings with the Marines. All he wanted to know was, "What did you tell them?"

"I told them I could do this."

My dad approved.

"Good!" he said.

"I'm not sure how I'm going to do this," I said nervously, "but I'm going to!"

"Don't worry," he reassured me, "you will figure it out and whatever you need I will be here to help you."

My father had always supported my endeavors, but I was entering uncharted territory. My father, a former street-smart businessman and always shrewd but a real gentleman, offered me a piece of advice that day that was pure gold.

He said, "I want you to find a lawyer who does trademarks and let's get you trademarked. Every idea you come up with, we'll stamp a trademark on it."

This wasn't just good fatherly advice; I had gotten burned not so long ago by the man for whom I'd made amazing children's face paint kits, who wanted to make money off my work. Now he wanted to make sure that MY work remained MY work.

The first trademark I secured was for Sports Fan Face Paint. He also wanted me to trademark my name, Bobbie Weiner, which I did and then Bobbie Weiner's Camouflage Face Paint.

ᏚᎦ ᏚᎦ ᏚᎦ ᏚᎦ ᏚᎦ

I had about four months to get all my college paint ready, and just two weeks to get back to the Marines with a new camouflage.

I bought some makeup from a huge cosmetics manufacturer and started experimenting. I put several trial formulas into containers that I had found at a drug store. To this day, the ingredients I use are all-natural and oil-free; they use no animal products and aren't tested on animals. They're mineral and pigment based, so they last a long time. All my makeup comes off with soap and water and doesn't stain skin.

To test the durability of the camouflage paint as I developed it, I asked some of the crew from Renegade who surfed to wear it while they rode the waves on La Jolla Beach. They gladly accepted the chance to surf in the name of research. I'd meet them on the beach at 4:30 a.m. to paint their faces, and they'd surf for 4 or 5 hours straight. I'd go get a cup of coffee and come back to check on them. We did this for two days. The camouflage didn't come off in the salt water, sand or sweat. It didn't irritate their skin. I'd met the challenge the military gave me — I was sure of it.

I went back to the military bases and met with the managers. Both wanted my camouflage. Camp Pendleton asked if I would paint the faces of their kids in the base's upcoming catalogue. Of course I agreed, and when MCRD asked me to do makeup for them on Halloween, I said "Absolutely!"

Then, another stroke of luck: the gentleman at MCRD told me about a military convention taking place in Dallas within three weeks. It was for Defense Logistics Agency, DLA, and was an international show that people came from all over the world to attend. The head of recruiting said, "You have to get a booth there and take samples." He offered to call on my behalf and see if they had an extra booth space. Three weeks later, Seth and I were on a plane heading for Dallas.

This time Seth was to be covered in camo paint. I had a 10-by-10 booth, the smallest at the show. But I'd read a thing or two about attracting people to my booth at these types of conventions. I rented a popcorn machine, knowing the smell of fresh popcorn would lure people my way. The popcorn machine took up almost half of the booth, shared with 200 samples of camo I had made by hand. I was nervous as could be and felt out of my element. This was a major gamble for me; the booth cost about $4,000 plus two rooms in a hotel and our meals — for four days.

By 1:30 p.m. the first day, the word about me and my new camouflage paint was out. It went just like the college show had. Even the popcorn guy started demo-ing the camo because the line was so long. Within four hours, we ran out of room and had to ditch the popcorn machine. Everyone wanted to meet the makeup lady who was developing a more durable camo face paint for the Marines. The head of recruiting at MCRD came by my booth.

When I looked up and saw him trying to get my attention, he gave me an enthusiastic "thumbs up". The line of customers waiting to talk with me was five people deep and 100 feet long.

There were the Army, the Marines, Navy and Special Forces and military people from all over the world.

I suddenly was like a one-woman USO! This was all promising, but I still hadn't actually sold anything to the military. To do that, I learned by the second day of the convention, I needed hard-to-come-by National Security Numbers (NSN) and a Commercial and Government Entity (CAGE) code. They're very, very hard to get (almost impossible, in fact, since the United States has been at war). But at the time, it mainly took major-league networking.

I would wander around the show asking people, "Who do I call for these numbers?" I stood outside the convention center, in the delivery parking lot, and spent hours on the phone, trying to talk to the right people. One person led to another. I didn't stop until I reached the point person who knew exactly what to do. That day, I racked up a $400 cell phone bill, and it was worth every dime.

Seth and I left that show the following afternoon with a very empty suitcase and a small arsenal of new contacts. Six weeks later my persistence paid off — I received my NSN numbers and my CAGE code. Now I was in the system; each time I came up with a new product after that, I could just call them up and pitch it to them without having to break through so much red tape.

The calls from the military came pouring in after that. My camouflage face paint was put in every new recruit's boot camp "goody" bag (along with things like shoe polish and a toothbrush.) In fact, each time the newscasters would announce that the United States was sending troops overseas, I knew about it because the order for camouflage had already been placed.

Chapter 7

Growing Pains

I soon discovered there was not a bank in town that would lend me money to start my little business. I went into a lending institute allegedly "friendly" to small women-owned businesses.

I presented a hard order from the Marines and orders from 46 colleges. It was a no-go — they would not lend me $10,000. In our meeting, the two bank executives asked me exactly what it would cost to create the makeup for colleges and the military. I told them to the penny, projected what the wholesale price would be and the approximate end user's price. They were shocked at my precision and knowledge, and told me they were very impressed.

"But, still no money..." I said.

Both of them had the balls to ask me to try to help get their kids into modeling, but they wouldn't give me any money! They were only thinking of themselves. I walked out — no way was I helping them.

Dejected but determined, I walked out and did what I had feared I would have to do: I drove up to L.A. and sold my 1987 Jeep Wrangler to a car dealer. I called my best friend and told her what I was doing. She owned four or five luxury cars — Mercedes, Jaguar and Rolls Royce — and urged me to take one. I said, "No way!" The events that followed set a memorable scene on the streets of L.A.

There I was, standing on the busiest corner of Ventura Boulevard with my steering wheel lock, A.K.A. "The Club," in one hand and a Louis Vuitton duffle bag at my feet, waiting for Enterprise Car Rental to pick me up. This was a humbling moment. No longer a car owner, my wallet held a check for $6,500 in its place. The driver pulled up, and an hour later I was heading back to San Diego in a very tiny car. It resembled an egg with a lot of glass and not much room, but I could lease it for $400 a month using my "sign and travel" credit card.

Determined to make my business work no matter what, I drove that tiny car for four months. I had to exchange it every month for the same model in a new color, until I spotted a little red Wrangler one day when passing a Jeep dealership in San Diego. It had neither air conditioning nor door locks, but it was an automatic transmission, so I called the dealership.

I figured it would be cheaper to buy a Jeep and make payments than to continue renting at $400 a month. I called the dealership and made and appointment with the manager. I told them over the phone that I wanted to buy the red Jeep in the parking lot, but I wasn't going to if I couldn't deal directly with the manager. Upon the advice of my lawyer, I arrived there with proof of income and my purchase order papers from the government and the colleges. I also brought in my divorce papers to show the manager I was not responsible for any of the credit cards, which still had high balances. I was not there to play the car game.

On this day, I had $1,200 in the bank. I was prepared to give it all to the manager in return for the Jeep, but he refused to take it. He said he didn't want to take the only money I had, so he made me a deal. I gave him $800 and he gave me four months to bring in another $1,200.

I left the rental car at this dealership and drove off in the Jeep I came for. True to my word, I went back four months later and paid what I owed. This deal felt like a huge victory and restored my faith in mankind after the terrible experiences I'd had trying to get bank loans.

ℭℭ ℭℭ ℭℭ ℭℭ ℭℭ

In mid-1997, I moved into high gear. I used the entire amount of money I received for my car — $6,500 — to get the blister cards made for Bobbie Weiner's Sports Fan Face Paint. At the same time, I was filling my camouflage order with a sub-contractor who was grateful for the business.

Like anyone trying to get a new business off the ground, I made my share of mistakes and encountered some surprises in the beginning. In July of that year, I shipped my first orders. I was using a small facility for packaging my Sports Fan makeup and everything was on schedule. At last — light shining at the end of the tunnel — until I received calls from Penn State and Louisiana State University. Their orders had gotten switched. Penn State had received purple and gold face paints, and LSU got navy and white. I called my packaging people and asked what happened.

Preparing to ship an order to Boston University, I asked the manager of the packaging company, "What colors are you sending to BU?"

He answered, "Green and gold."

Stunned, I said, "Their colors are maroon and gold." As a joke, I added, "Are you color blind?"

He replied cautiously, "Well, not really…just sometimes."

"What do you mean, 'sometimes'?" I asked incredulously.

"I just have trouble with pinks and gray," he told me.

"I think you have trouble with blue and maroon and purple, also," I said.

I couldn't believe I'd hired a man who was color-blind to package my face paint orders — a job whose chief requirement was to get the colors right!

Just a week earlier, I had done this guy a huge favor: he was getting married and I did his bride's makeup. I also did the mother of the bride, the bridesmaids — everybody involved in the wedding — all for free. And now this guy was completely screwing up my business, not to mention my bottom line!

I called the man who had manufactured my Sports Fan cards, as he had suggested the packer who was color blind. This man would not give me credit four months earlier when I tried to get him to make my cards. He was the reason I was forced to sell my car. I said, "Hey, you have got to help me find another packaging source. Do you know anyone else who could help me?"

I needed to do something, and fast. The orders were rolling in, and I had to get them filled on time. And accurately.

When I had told him about the color-blind packing manager, he was sort of amused. I was not amused. Knowing that I was on to something, he told me about another man in San Diego who might help. I followed up immediately and called a man named Jim; within 24 hours he had moved my stock from the color-blind guy's packaging facility into his sizable facility in National City.

Jim straightened out everything, providing all that was necessary to run my business smoothly. This man was the best! He enabled my business to grow and become the success it is today. A Vietnam vet, Jim did contract work for the government and took me under his wing, teaching me how to work the business. His philosophy was, "If you own a restaurant and your dish washer doesn't show, you'd better know how to wash the dishes." I was about to learn how to do everything.

I started with how to operate every machine. He was a great teacher — so knowledgeable and humble, as if he had all of the time in the world for me. Estranged from his family and grown children, Jim's company consumed his life, but he had become successful and bored. When I entered his life, we became best friends. I warehoused everything at his factory and opened my first little showroom in La Jolla.

Outside of work, Jim had a fabulous girlfriend and they became my San Diego family. We ate dinner every Tuesday night at the cheap chicken wing place and shared brunch on Sunday mornings. I felt so lucky to have met them. I believe things happen for a reason: If the first packer had not been color blind, our paths would never have crossed. What a wonderful mentor Jim turned out to be.

∞ ∞ ∞ ∞ ∞

Back then, I thought I would be rich within one year. My dad told me to give myself five years. I was not happy to hear that information, but I kept working and growing Bobbie Weiner Enterprises. A few clients met with me in my 200-square foot office in La Jolla, affectionately christened "The Closet." I was never ashamed of the size of my office. It was mine and I paid my bills. I did not care about size, just my ability to offer the best products made in the U.S.A. and deliver on time. Attendees visiting my exhibits at the military shows consistently raved, "You have the smallest space, but the mightiest booth in all of the show."

∞ ∞ ∞ ∞ ∞

On Dec. 19, 1997, Titanic hit the big screen and the world went nuts. I didn't get to go to any premieres, and I wasn't even credited on screen because the makeup department was so huge and I had only came in and for special effects work for a short time. However, my name was on every call sheet under "makeup department," so there was proof that I'd worked on it!

49

But it didn't matter. The fact that I was even connected to this block-buster would attract phenomenal attention. I continued to pitch my story to every news outlet I could think of to try to help generate business.

My memories of my ex-husband were long gone by this time. In five years, I had reinvented myself, found a career (which I was actually good at) and launched my own business. I was no longer The Doctor's Wife. I was Bobbie Weiner, a.k.a. Bloody Mary, a.k.a. "The Makeup Lady."

Little did I know that I was about to "pay it forward" and that my life's story might start to help other people.

ഇ ഇ ഇ ഇ ഇ

About 6 months after the movie came out, the San Diego newspaper did a story on me — an entire front-page spread in the business section in which I talked all about my background and how I got into my career. A woman in Rancho Santa Fe, one the wealthiest San Diego suburbs, read the article and looked me up. Turns out her husband, too, had just left her, taken everything and knocked up his younger girlfriend down the street. This woman didn't want to know anything about painting dead people; she wanted to know how to survive.

She invited me to speak to a woman's group at Scripps Mercy Hospital in San Diego, in a fundraising event where they served champagne and chocolate-dipped strawberries.

At the beginning of the evening, I was standing behind one of the poles outside the hospital and a woman approached me.

"Are you Bobbie?" she asked. "I was washing the dishes and a promotion for this event came on the news and I told my husband, 'You finish the dishes, I'm going to meet this lady. I've got to go there.'" And she called her best friend. They came immediately, and the two of them wanted my autograph. They paid $45 apiece to hear me speak, which I could hardly believe.

They weren't the only ones. The auditorium filled up; you could have heard a pin drop, the women were so silent and attentive. I was every woman's nightmare: that the husband would leave for a younger woman. I was that statistic that they didn't ever want to deal with. I wasn't shopping or playing tennis anymore; I had been to the living hell that they didn't ever want to visit. There were some pretty big-name local celebrities in the crowd. I wore my good-luck cowboy hat; they wore their good Prada and Chanel.

I had not done much public speaking, but I spoke about how I started the business, basically from nothing. They gave me a microphone and put a chair onstage and I was so uncomfortable. When I said I couldn't do it on stage, they brought it down to the audience. I spoke for an hour, which surprised me most of all!

I'll never forget the scene immediately after the event, when people lined up at the valet stand for their cars...you name a luxury car, and it was being brought around. Not too long ago, I had been one of these rich wives, waiting for my fancy ride, a hot Porsche convertible. As the valet guy brought my little red ragtop Jeep around, all eyes were on me. One of the snobby women said, condescendingly, "Is that your car? Isn't that adorable!" But I didn't care at all.

The same lady who had arranged that event then organized a luncheon at the Rancho Santa Fe Country Club. She charged a fortune, and some pretty big-name people showed up; in fact, they hired security for the event because of all the jewelry the women were wearing.

This woman — the one whose husband had left her for the girlfriend down the street and had taken everything — told me she had to get a job now and had no idea where to start.

"What are you good at?" I asked her.

She said, "I know how to run a house."

"There are so many wealthy people around here, that shouldn't be a problem," I said. I wasn't joking; I was dead serious.

She said, "I saw an ad in the classifieds. There's a guy who has a home in San Francisco (where he lived for most of the year), and they need someone to keep the house here in La Jolla while they're there. It pays $50,000 a year." She wouldn't have to live there; she'd just have to hire a cook and a housekeeper and run the house for 2 or 3 weeks out of the year.

I said, "Are you kidding me? You run for that job!"

It ended up being a $22 million house. The mysterious owner who'd put the ad in the paper? None other than Microsoft titan Bill Gates.

That woman adored me. She couldn't believe she had gotten this job to manage somebody's house, and Bill Gates of all people!

I was gratified by the fact that my story could help other women. Women need to feel empowered. They need their own identity, and I was living, breathing proof of someone who'd lost mine and then found a new one.

Even today, when I speak to women's groups and to female students on college campuses, I always tell them, "You've got to have your own thing going on. If he's blue and you're green when you meet, you stay green; don't let him turn you blue."

ᘒᘓ ᘒᘓ ᘒᘓ ᘒᘓ ᘒᘓ

In January 1998, just as I was riding the Titanic crest, the Downtown San Diego Chamber of Commerce invited me to be featured at the upcoming Super Bowl in San Diego. They were showcasing the Best of San Diego and had chosen my company because I was a very small company with a big resume. They appreciated the fact that my Sports Fan Face Paint was produced locally, and my corporation was based in San Diego.

I ended up getting prime corner space for my Super Bowl exhibit, located on a city block in the historic Gas Lamp District. I found eight people to help run the booth and we were right smack next to the Budweiser space. We rocked! I painted faces for free but took tips and enlisted two other face painters who kept their tips, as well. People waited up to two hours to get their faces and bodies painted, and we sold the kits in the colors of the two teams competing — the Denver Broncos and Green Bay Packers. We worked around the clock from 6:00 p.m. Friday, nonstop Saturday until early Sunday morning, until we had sold out — we were elated and exhausted!

I handed out thousands of Sports Fan business cards, the best possible advertising for my business. Soon after the Super Bowl, calls came in from high schools and colleges from all over the country, from sports fans who had never heard of Bloody Mary or Bobbie Weiner Enterprises. We got busier than ever.

I ran my business from the tiny "closet" office for two years, until I could afford to move into a 500 square-foot space; boy, I thought I was living the high life then! Jim hired an operations manager and basically ran the whole operation from his warehouse in National City.

I was still out there "pounding the pavement" — putting a face to a name behind the company. On weekends, I would paint football fans' faces for three hours before the Chargers games outside their stadium. During the long baseball season, I'd do the same thing at the Padres games. By doing that I got 4 seats to every game, but I usually gave them away. They'd put my name on the marquee, saying something like: "Thank you to Bobbie Weiner Sports Fan Face Paint." This was the BEST possible advertising I could have imagined. Then the Padres went to the World Series against the New York Yankees in October 1998, and we worked 24 hours a day.

I scored another huge sports coup, also in 1998: The World Cup, the international soccer tournament (you know — the one the rest of the world calls "football.") In the summer of '98, it was being held in France. A distributor of ladies' makeup had read about my Sports Fan Face Paint

Kits in the La Jolla newspaper and contacted me about getting them in the French team's colors of red, white and blue.

They didn't want to sell my products; they just wanted to offer face painting to French soccer fans outside the stadium. No problem, right? Red, white and blue aren't exactly the most exotic colors to come up with. Why was he seeking me out when there were a ton of other makeup providers around the world he could have gone to?

It was the quality of my paint, I soon learned. To be able to use face paint in France, it must pass rigorous testing in French hospitals. You have to get it to a hospital, where they examine and test it thoroughly to make sure it doesn't harm the skin. My stuff was good enough for the United States military, this guy thought — it should pass French biology tests. And it did.

We got pushed up against a one-month deadline, but I sold him enough paint for 40,000 to 50,000 face paint kits. Special blister cards were printed in French and a company in Europe put all the kits together. We got paid up front for all of this, and even though it paid less than $10,000 outright, the fact that we were now reaching internationally was amazing, I thought.

Business kept expanding toward the end of the '90s; we were soon making our own compacts and injection molds. This was a big deal because injection molds were expensive to make, and I was proud to be doing it in the United States. People advised me it would be much cheaper to send the operation overseas, to someplace like China, and I did actually explore this idea.

I set up two different conference calls with an interpreter in Washington, D.C. on one end and a person in China on the other. Both times, I stayed up until 2:30 in the morning — the time the calls were made. Both times, no one answered. These international conference calls were expensive to organize. After the second time no one answered, I was done. My business was staying in America. To this day, I'm proud to say, every aspect of the business is done in the U.S.A.

Chapter 8

Big Gains and a Terrible Loss

I was still living with people a couple years into running the business, but I was paying the bills, and to me, that was success. I wasn't even thinking of dating; my business was my new spouse. I was giving it one thousand percent of my time, day and night. Who had time for a social life?

In early 1999, I found out — by accident — about a huge Halloween and party trade show in Chicago that reps and buyers for party stores, costume shops and haunted houses around the world would be attending. I had called a customer about Sports Fan Face Paint kits, and he asked, "Aren't you going to be at the Halloween show?" He gave the contact phone number, I called, and the man in charge faxed me back that he'd had a cancellation and now had booth space for me. The show was six weeks away.

On the application, I mentioned that I made up the Titanic people. I casually sent that form off with credit card information to secure the booth; not five minutes later, the show coordinator called and said the event planner for the show wanted to speak to me. She was having a luncheon for haunted house professionals and still didn't have guest speaker. Would I do a Titanic-style dead-person demo on stage? Of course! At this point, Titanic was old news to me, but, hey — if it helped this woman out AND helped me sell face paint, I was more than willing to help.

I was beyond excited about this show. So was my father. Sol had never wanted to attend a big show like this before, but he thought the haunted house one would be great fun. I even got him credentials to get in. Unfortunately, he never got the chance to wear them.

Sol suffered a heart attack and died in Florida just three weeks before the show. I was utterly and completely devastated; my father had been not just my "daddy" but my guiding light, my touchstone, my role model in my newfound career. He always believed in me, always supported me, and always gave me wise business advice on matters I wouldn't have ever thought of — trademarking my name, for example.

My dad believed that above all else, you should be a nice person, and he lived true to that creed. "If you're a nice person and you become successful," he'd tell me, "you'll become an even nicer person. But if you're a no-good bastard and you become successful, you'll just become an even bigger no-good bastard."

Solomon Weiner was my hero in every way possible.

As a tradition, before I attend any trade show now, I get two extra badges: one for my mom, and one for my dad. I often let people use them if they want to see what the show is like. It's a nice gesture, and it's something my dad would have done.

Still grieving for my father, I went to the Halloween show in Chicago in early March of 1999. My mother flew there, too — the first time she'd ever flown alone in her life — because I thought she needed to get out and try to have a good time after my father's death. People there knew we'd just suffered a terrible loss, and they treated my mother like gold. I was so grateful.

This show ended up becoming another career-defining experience for me. On the stage while people were eating lunch, I did a Titanic demo on one of my reps. During my talk, I happened to tell the crowd, "They call me Bloody Mary." Afterwards, people were taking pictures of me and following me around like I was the Pied Piper… it was "Mary this" and "Mary that."

A guy with a horror magazine asked if he could interview me. As I made him into a frozen corpse, he asked me questions, among them, "What's the best Halloween makeup out there?" Almost without thinking, I said, "My own makeup, Bloody Mary." I told him I made death makeup and blood and setting powders. So he wrote that, and Bloody Mary makeup was born. (There I went again, telling someone I could do something and then having to figure out how to get it done!)

Haunted house reps started asking what I would charge to visit their houses and train their actors to do makeup. First I said, "$1,800 and you pay my plane and hotel;" then it went up to $2,000, then $2,500. I couldn't believe people were willing to pay so much for my services!

I left that show and went back to San Diego to start making Bloody Mary death makeup and blood, as I'd promised my new-found fans. My blood wouldn't contain any sugars, I decided, remembering back to my Renegade days when, after fight scenes, I'd have to completely redo the actors' makeup because they were covered in sticky, heavy, gross fake blood; it was the consistency of Karo syrup and would actually attract bugs and bees and ants!

Bloody Mary blood still doesn't contain any sugars and it washes off with soap and water. I still tell everyone I meet, "I make the best blood. I'm KNOWN for my blood!"

In June of 1999, Bobbie Weiner Enterprises received the first of two gold medals from the United States Department of Defense. I still consider these awards the most important I have ever received. I keep the letters announcing the medals in a notebook along with dozens of newspaper clippings, and I have the photos of the awards ceremony hanging on the walls of my office. The awards are actually called Automated Best Value System medals and are awarded to government contractors whose products meet "stringent quality, price and delivery requirements established by the Defense Logistics Agency and are eligible for bid preference when competing for future government contracts," the agency says.

In '99, I was one of 300 contractors who received the honor. That may not sound too prestigious, until you think that the Defense Supply Center in Richmond, Va., which awarded the medal, managed more than 750,000 items used by the military and other government agencies that year.

I flew to Richmond to accept the medal and was stunned to be one of only three women who were getting the award that year. Surrounded by hundreds of men in the room, I was feeling ignored already. Then I went ahead and stuck my foot in my mouth and said something that was sure to alienate me for the rest of the evening. I turned to one of the men in uniform and asked, "What kind of costume is he wearing?" referring to another distinguished man in a very decorated United States Military uniform. To this day, I cringe each time I think about what a dumbass I must have sounded like. It's shocking that they gave me another gold medal just three years later, in 2002. I thought for sure I would have "black balled" myself from receiving any future awards from the United States military!

ೞ ೞ ೞ ೞ ೞ

When I returned from Richmond that summer, I was riding high from the military honor. But what came next was even more expected. I was approached by Comic-Con International through Lloyd Kaufman, a producer out of New York and Los Angeles and the owner of Troma Entertainment. I had never heard of Troma, or, believe it or not, of Comic-Con.

Lloyd was lining up guest speakers for Comic-Con in San Diego the next Saturday and asked me to give a presentation. He said that he'd read about me, and his people knew my reputation and my work. Troma Entertainment films featured horror and soft porn themes, and he explained that he wanted to present me as the guest speaker to "class up" his organization.

I had never been to a comic book convention, but he wanted me to talk about my experience with Hollywood and present makeup demos onstage using models and volunteers from the audience. He knew I was a local, and living in San Diego made it an easy commitment for me.

I arrived early that Saturday, amazed by the traffic and the lengthy Comic-Con admission line that seemed to stretch down to Mexico. More than 120,000 people showed up! Lloyd had posted my name in front of the convention center. I was speechless and overwhelmed.

Lloyd took me to the auditorium where I would be speaking. It held over 4,000 people and two of his most notorious characters, Toxic Avenger and The Kabuki Man, welcomed me onto the huge stage up front. They were hysterical and I sat wedged between them. This was already surreal to me.

The audience started pouring in, and within a half hour the auditorium was filled to capacity — standing room only. At least one-third of the audience wore theater makeup and costumes, a great representation of every big action movie ever made along with every imaginative character ever created. Some had fashioned their own outrageous styles; what an audience I was about to speak to!

I gave my "Bloody Mary" presentation for an hour, then asked for volunteers. No problem getting any in this audience. This was my kind of crowd — I was so charged up. The audience sat mesmerized. I received a standing ovation at the end of that amazing experience. As the crowd waited in line for my autograph, I knew I had to be part of their world.

I went for coffee, found a spot on the floor and watched a passionate parade of comic fans march by me. Then I stepped into the convention center and a sea of exhibit booths. It was enormous — the biggest convention I'd ever seen — even bigger than the military convention in Dallas. I started asking people who the biggest distributor of comic books was and made a beeline for that booth. I met the branding manager for Diamond Comics and told him I wanted to create a comic book. Fortunately, he had attended my presentation earlier that day and simply said, "Good, here is my card. Send me your comic book when you're done."

I walked the show a little more, stopped a few times to sign autographs, went to the Troma booth and thanked Lloyd for inviting me to be part of such an amazing event. I walked six blocks to my car and drove back to my office, where I created a character named "Mary" and a storyline called "The Tales of Bloody Mary."

Let me say here that even with all of this "Bloody Mary" character stuff, I had never heard of the legend of Bloody Mary — the one that says if you say her name three times in the dark, in front of a mirror, she appears. People ask me all the time if that's a part of my shtick as Bloody Mary, and I tell them the honest truth: that I was entirely unaware of that legend when I was developing my Bloody Mary persona and products. So, no, it never has been part of my shtick and it never will be.

That same afternoon, after my Comic-Con appearance, I applied makeup to myself, transforming my face into a horrific monster. I took photos of my handiwork and had them developed the following day. A young UCSD student who worked for me part-time took the negative and imposed a gargoyle on my head; then we placed the photo on a jumbo postcard. I refined my story and created a prototype postcard, which I sent to the brand manager at Diamond Comic Distributors. A week or two later, he called and invited me to appear in his Comic-Con booth the following year.

"Bring a couple thousand postcards to sign and plan on being there one to two hours," he instructed. This comic book thing was really going to happen! At that point, I knew I needed an artist, someone who could really draw and capture the look I envisioned for my character.

That took some doing, but in 2000, I made my second appearance at Comic-Con. Diamond and I produced a gorgeous display, drawing a line of fans that seemed to stretch forever. To attract attention to my booth (I'd gotten good at this after all the shows I'd done to this point), I made a woman to look like a Titanic corpse and had her hand out postcards and encourage people to get in line for autographs.

My Bloody Mary product line generated all kinds of excitement — it was fantastic. I had brought haunt makeup, including my kick-ass blood, and had even designed a "Bloody Mary" lunchbox that people could carry the makeup in. The stuff was selling left and right!

Every piece was falling into place, but I still needed to develop the real thing, a comic book. A few prospective illustrators come and went, but no one took my offer seriously. I knew there were a lot of talented people who could really draw, but I needed someone who would return my calls and who would not disappear on me. It would take some more time to find the perfect artist — but eventually, I did.

Chapter 9

A Big Move

In the midst of competitive demands and the rising success of my company, my mother, Betty, fell ill in March 2001. I flew to Florida to learn what was wrong and discovered she had lung cancer. She also still struggled with the loss of my dad, who had passed away two years earlier. My dad's death was sudden; he suffered a heart attack one night and it was over. My mother really never came to terms with the fact that he was gone. Dad did everything in our family and had taken care of her since she was a girl of 13.

She was helpless now and I became her caretaker, still living 3,000 miles away in San Diego. I had to be there for my mother. People told me, "Why don't you put her in a nursing home?" I said, "You put your mother in a nursing home; mine will never see one."

Striving to keep my promising new business on track, I arranged for someone to live with my mother, take her to medical appointments and generally serve as her companion. Every Friday night I took a red-eye flight from San Diego to Fort Lauderdale, and every Monday morning at 5:30 a.m. I flew back to California. I did that for four months, and finally the pace became too much. I saw two choices: to bring my terminally ill mother to California or to move to Florida and re-establish my business there. I could not bring myself to move mother out of her home, separating her from longtime friends and everything familiar, so I adjusted my life for her.

It was an overnight move for me. Professional packers boxed up my entire office and, at a cost of $15,000 for the shipping alone, set up shop in Fort Lauderdale by 10 a.m. the next day. It was a scorching, sticky day in August 2001.

I still provided someone to stay with my mother all day so I could work, but I slept at her home every night, commuting once or twice a month to California. As so many people do, I became the mother in our relationship. Knowing her days were numbered, I was determined to make her life as good as I could right up to the end, and I did.

I arranged 24-hour care in her own place, literally transforming her bedroom into a hospital room. I do not know where and how I found the strength, but you just do, I guess.

ରୋ ରୋ ରୋ ରୋ ରୋ

In the midst of my mother's health crisis and my sudden move cross country, I had to operate a makeup company with all of the growing pains that accompany a small business with big ideas.

Somewhere in all the chaos that summer, I got a call from a bank president in Massachusetts. Five investors wanted to invest $100,000 each in my business. They wanted a total of 20 percent of just the camouflage portion of Bobbie Weiner Enterprises. Half a million dollars sounded great to me!

The banker said he needed to get a prospectus for each potential investor, so I provided a portfolio for each one. They changed their offer.

They wanted to each invest $100,000 to own 20 percent of the entire company — not just the camouflage division.

I insisted it would cost them more than that — about $250,000 each. After I made that offer, I never heard from them again. Their silence was the best thing that ever happened to me — and a mistake for them — because Bobbie Weiner Enterprises was about to go places no one could have imagined, after Sept. 11, 2001.

ᎾᏏ ᎾᏏ ᎾᏏ ᎾᏏ ᎾᏏ

The terrorist attacks on 9/11 changed my life — and my business — for good. I was at the bank when I heard that a plane hit one of the World Trade Center towers; I decided the office needed a television, so I drove to Circuit City, and by the time I got there, people were gathered around large TV sets, watching replays of both the first and the second plane crash.

I dashed back to the office, plugged the TV in and stayed glued to it that day. "Something big is going to happen here," my employees and I were telling ourselves. "We need to get ready."

We were right. Within two weeks, the orders for camouflage face paint came pouring in. Business from the Department of Defense tripled. Our camouflage, remember, was given to all the new military recruits when they started boot camp, and enlistments were skyrocketing across the nation as young men and women signed up to defend our country.

Bobbie Weiner Enterprises became a seemingly tiny yet utterly indispensible part of the new military operations in Afghanistan and then Iraq. It was unbelievable.

As the terrorist attacks led to full-blow military operations in the Middle East, Americans' interest — and the media's coverage — of all topics military-related became insatiable. This included, believe it or not, the topic of camouflage face paint. I got a call that CNN wanted to interview me, and on December 4, 2001, they patched me in from my office in Miami for a one-on-one interview.

The broadcaster, Pat Kiernan, asked me how I made the transition from being a Hollywood makeup artist to a supplier of camouflage face paint to the military, so I condensed my story — starting with Titanic — into a quick, sound bite-length answer.

I was also asked what it was like to approach the military as a female in business. I said it wasn't as hard as you might think, that "it's like anything else. If you get the right people at the right time, it just happens." The interview was fairly short, but it was just another in a long list of experiences I absolutely couldn't believe I was having now. The Doctor's Wife certainly would never have had the opportunity to be on CNN!

Every time since 9/11 that the U.S. military has sent a surge a soldiers and Marines to war, I've known about it ahead of time because there's been a surge in orders for camouflage face paint. It's an honor to fill those orders.

ᘓᗝ ᘓᗝ ᘓᗝ ᘓᗝ ᘓᗝ

Hollywood also took notice of me again. By the early 2000s, I wasn't doing makeup for movies anymore, but I began supplying it for films. When 20th Century Fox was filming the movie Behind Enemy Lines starring Owen Wilson and Gene Hackman (released in November 2001), the makeup artist called because they needed special effects makeup to make actors look like dead, frozen military men. And because they were shooting the action thriller in frigid Slovakia and it was filled with all sorts of stunts and acrobatics, they needed good makeup that wouldn't wear off in harsh conditions.

They sent the script to me so I could break it down and see what their needs would be, and I shipped a haul of makeup to the studio. They ran out halfway through the shooting, and one night they called me at 3 a.m. for some more. The movie did very well at the box office and is still a favorite among fans of military action flicks. All the special effects makeup came from Bobbie Weiner Enterprises. There's even a scene where all the guys take out camo and put it on, and that's ours, too.

That was the first film we supplied makeup for; we do a lot of them now. Anytime you watch a military movie in which camouflage is used, we may not be credited, but you can almost safely guess that it came from Bobbie Weiner.

ॐ ॐ ॐ ॐ ॐ

My mother, Betty, died in my arms in 2002. She was a remarkably funny, lively woman, right until the end. I sometimes felt I let my mother down; her biggest dream for me was to get married and have children. Well, I got married all right. Plenty of times. But the children never came, and if I have a single regret in life, it's that I never had children.

My mother had a wicked sense of humor. On the mantel of my parents' Florida home, she kept a framed photo of her and my dad with my first husband and me. Each time I got married, rather than replace the whole photo, she'd cut out the head of the new husband and place him on the body of the old one. I didn't even know she was doing this until my father announced to me one night that my mother was "doing some artwork," and that was her little project.

If my father taught me to be a nice person, my mother taught me to give back. She often told me that whatever I gave to other people I'd get back in return, at least double. That is her legacy to me. Well, that and the fact that her illness forced me to move to Florida, where I met one of the most important people to my business: Tom Carlton.

I always said, "My mother brought me to Florida for two reasons: to care and be there for her and to meet Tom, who became my artist and right hand in the business."

ᥩᥩ ᥩᥩ ᥩᥩ ᥩᥩ ᥩᥩ

This is how I met Tom: right after I made the move to Florida in 2001, I needed business cards and printing supplies, so I scouted out a printer close to my office. Needing to get "The Tales of Bloody Mary" comic book out of my head and down on paper, I asked if anyone at the print shop knew someone who could do animation artwork.

The lady at the front desk writing up my order said, "Tommy. He is really quite good."

"Who is Tommy?" I asked.

She replied, "He works in the back."

I asked her to give him my telephone number. Tom called me that evening and came in to meet me the following day. He showed me his work and I gave him my storyline and an idea what I was looking for. Soon he returned with 8 pages, black and white, and he nailed it. That was the beginning of our working relationship, the creation of my comic book and his dream.

"Zombie Tom" stayed head of the art department for the print shop and worked for me for a year, as well. When we finally completed the first prototype for "Tales of Bloody Mary," I sent it overnight express to Diamond Industries, my distributor-to-be. Within 24 hours, they called and said, "This is great!"

The branding manager was very enthusiastic and offered one or two suggestions:

"Tone down the blood a little, mute out the colors and you will have yourself a hit." (There I was being heavy-handed again, just like I'd been in makeup school!)

Tom and I worked together with the branding manager for almost another year until our prototype was acceptable to Diamond; then we were off and running in 2002. I took a chance and printed 100 copies for a Halloween Horror Convention — we sold every one. We actually ran out of them. We also sold out at Comic-Con in 2003. We had a hit on our hands!

The character of Bloody Mary is a 17-year-old young woman who died prematurely and now haunts the earth influencing evil. It is a horror book with a bit of goth, and the character's mysterious story unfolds with each edition.

A review of the first "Tales of Bloody Mary" in a trade publication applauded its script and art, saying "there's definitely more ... than meets the eye." It went on to say, "Funny thing about this launch issue is that it dangles T&A and S&M left, right and center, but constantly reigns itself in and makes actual efforts to seed a damn plot!"

In an interview, Tom — who is an Art Institute graduate and an amazing artist — said Mary could be hard to draw because she was so multi-faceted ... horrific at times and beautiful at others, confused and scared yet strong.

Leave it to me to create a character that complex! The fact is, once we had Bloody Mary from the comic book, she was able to take our business in all kinds of new directions. She's already done a lot for us, and she continues to evolve.

Chapter 10

A Change in Priorities

My business was still growing when I was living in Florida, but I was by no means getting rich. Every dime I was getting I was putting right back into the company. All the conventions and trade shows I was going to were costing me a fortune — the average show costs about $10,000 when it's said and done — but they were paying off because I was attracting distributors who were selling my stuff around the country. (To give some context, it probably cost me a total of $100,000 to find a distributor to get my makeup sold in Wal-Mart.)

If I didn't come away with a distributor at a show, I made some kind of contact or connection that would eventually help me. I believed in those shows and was doing 12 to 15 a year, sometimes every two to three weeks. Still, when you're selling products for $4.99 and $7.99 and $9.99, you've got to sell a heck of a lot of them to be turning a profit.

By most people's standards, I was still living a meager life. I'd lived with people in their homes for five years, and it wasn't until I moved to Florida that I got my own place. Sort of. After my mother died, I rented a fully-furnished, gorgeous apartment on the beach from my friend whose husband was the accountant for a horse trainer. (Everyone was into horse racing in Florida, it seemed.) This place was gorgeous, and I felt like I was living the high life again.

But I wanted to be closer to the office, so I got my own place. Tom, who began working for me full time, gathered and moved my clothes — that's all I had because the other place was furnished. I am not exaggerating when I say I had nothing. Not even plates or pillows of my own.

I left my office at the usual time of 8:00 the night I moved, and as I drove to my new place, it hit me: I didn't have a bed! I didn't have a lamp, I didn't have dishes, I had nothing.

I called my best friend Mary and said, "I don't know what I'm gonna sleep on tonight!" She told me to go to Bed, Bath & Beyond and to buy an Aerobed that I could plug into the wall to blow up. I got the Aerobed, and then realized I didn't have sheets or pillows. I had to call my friend Barbara and ask for an extra set of sheets. Another friend gave me toilet paper. I was so excited to have my own place, but I had nothing inside! It was totally un-livable! I went to the store and bought a couple of lamps so I could see. I ended up sleeping on that Aerobed for almost two years. (Hey, it was the greatest! I never had a neck ache or a backache!)

A fire department that I'd done a big fundraiser for gave me a fireman's blanket, so that kept me warm at night. These things just weren't important to me. I didn't care.

My friends and I had season tickets for the Miami Dolphins games, and I bought two ultra-cheap tailgate chairs at a drugstore. I didn't just tailgate in these chairs; they became my living room furniture, too. I'd sit in one of these low-to-the-ground chairs and watch my little 9-inch television at night. Hey, it was my life — who cared?

Turns out, my friends did. I'd won some tickets to a Chris Evert tennis event and invited friends over before the tournament one day. My friend

Mary took one look at those tailgate chairs and saw how I was living, and she started crying. She was hysterical. She was so upset for me.

She said, "Bobbie, you can't live like this!"

I said, "What's a matter? It doesn't matter to me!"

Mary thought I was pathetic. She went out and bought me dishes since I was still using paper plates. I did eventually buy some furnishings and house wares at the thrift shop because I ended up living in this apartment a few more years. I finally broke down and bought myself a real bed, too.

Maybe it did seem pathetic, but here's the thing: once everything was taken away after my divorce, my priorities changed. I didn't NEED nice stuff because nice stuff didn't make me happy. Plus, I'd lived with other people for so long as I launched my business that I just didn't have to buy a lot of stuff for myself. It was easy.

And then there was the practical matter that I was traveling like crazy when I was living in Florida.

ꙮ ꙮ ꙮ ꙮ ꙮ

In the early 2000s, I did a lot of guest speaking at conventions — some bigger than others, but all valuable appearances to help market my business. One of the biggest speaking gigs I got was for a major corporation, 7-Eleven convenience stores. I returned to Dallas, this time giving the keynote address on opening day for the 7-Eleven International Convention. More than 2,000 people attended – owners of 7-Eleven stores all around the world. What an honor!

The president of 7-Eleven introduced me and I basically presented the same program I gave for opening day at Comic-Con: I brought people up on the stage, transformed them into frozen, dead zombies and it was a big hit.

My exhibit booth sat next to a man who sold ice and Ben and Jerry's

Ice Cream, directly across from the Oscar Meyer Weiner truck. That show was an absolute food frenzy and a whole lot of fun. It paid off for me, too. We started selling face paint kits in 7-Eleven stores all over.

Part of the reason I had a blast at this convention was that I got to hang out with the wrestlers from the World Wrestling Federation. I had done the (formerly WCW) wrestlers' makeup a few years earlier, but this was a crop of all new guys, including a few big wigs from the organization.

The first night of this show, after I'd spoken, the convention folks drove us all to Billy Bob's for dinner and entertainment. I sat with Vince McMahon's (the owner of WWF) marketing manager on the bus on the way to Billy Bob's. I ate with him, and the wrestling crew, at Billy Bob's and we were joined by the hilarious "What's Up" boys from the Budweiser commercials.

After we ate, I said, "Why don't we play pool?" I don't even play pool — I was awful at it — but it gave us all something fun to do together. John, the WWF marketing man, and I became friends that night. We have kept in touch since, and I have supported his different causes and he has supported me.

John encouraged me to go to a big international licensing show, and to start marketing Bloody Mary by putting her name on more than just makeup and comic books.

I never knew which direction the company might go in next; doors opened and I walked through them. In 2002, a funeral director approached me about providing some makeup to his funeral home. This made sense, of course — funeral homes needed makeup, too. So I reformulated my line called "The Other Makeup" ("TOM" — which I was marketing to women to make them look younger). I made this makeup heavier and sent it to him. He replied with a check and a note: "Send me more." Again, I thought I might be onto something with this, so I relabeled and branded this line "Bloody Mary's The Final Touch."

Now we supply it to funeral homes all over the country and sell it in a variety of skin tones. We also sell jaundice powder and embalming filler (for filling in things like wounds, surgery scars and bullet holes). Believe it or not, young people started buying these products to look like real corpses in haunted houses.

Chapter 11

'Bloody Mary' Gets Hot - and Spicy

I was reluctant to go to the International Licensing Expo. It was in New York, and it was expensive — at $20,000, it was double the cost of most of the other shows we went to.

But the wrestlers from WWE kept encouraging me, so I bit the bullet and registered for the 2004 licensing show. We made prototypes of skateboards, piñatas, a bustier, gloves, hats, hoodies, shot glasses, koozies, jewelry — anything I could think of to stamp "Bloody Mary" on and get the name out there. We were now selling her. The comic book was selling through Diamond, the makeup was selling, and now, this would bring it all together.

This show ended up being great fun, too. The WWE booth was maybe 50 feet away from me; they sent some of the old-timers to sit in my booth, so we had a double-booth at the end of the aisle. We had two tables on either side, so we made it look like we were as big as life.

One of the most interesting people who walked up to our booth declared, "I want to make Bloody Mary hot sauce." What a great idea!

Some people collect hot sauce bottles like they're Kewpie Dolls (but a lot less valuable). After the show, I asked the WWE guys what they thought about this hot sauce possibility; they said, "Do it yourself. You'll never see money from that guy." So that's what we did — once again venturing into territory I knew nothing about ... I didn't even like hot sauce!

No one had ever trademarked the name "Bloody Mary" for sauces. Before the show was even over, I'd called my attorney and suggested we trademark it. Six months later, we got the trademark.

We found a marvelous hot sauce maker to private label bottles for us; he gave us different samples to try, and the guys in my company had a great time taste-testing. In a genius cross-promotional effort, we made the cover of our comic books the labels for the hot sauces. Now people collect ours (we have five different flavors) along with all the other hot sauces on their shelves!

When we went to Comic-Con in 2005, we took the hot sauce with us and sold every single one. The comic book distributor got them placed in comic book stores, too. We did limited edition labels for Halloween, Christmas and Valentine's Day and started packaging it in a black coffin box. We have added the annual hot sauce convention in Albuquerque to our list of regular conventions, and it's great fun.

About a year after the hot sauce took off, someone suggested we sell Bloody Mary mix. Of course! Why didn't I think of that? Our "hot sauce people" recommended Bloody Mary mix-makers, and the idea would be to put comic book labels on these, too. Again, I called my lawyer and suggested we trademark "Bloody Mary" Bloody Mary mix. He laughed. He didn't think we'd actually get this trademark, but we did — and now no one else can use our name or likeness on their Bloody Mary mix.

I'm not a drinker, but I do love Bloody Marys. I couldn't wait to taste-test the different mixes we might put our name on. So it must have been some bad karma when I came down with a sinus infection the day of the taste-test. With a sinus infection, you can't taste anything. I decided to give the mixes to my friend in Miami who owned a restaurant, she tested them out on her patrons. They did a great job tasting because, to this day, we get all kinds of compliments on the mix and consistently sell out of it.

They sell the hot sauce in the PX's on Army bases, and when I visit the bases, they ship even more bottles so I can autograph them in person.

You don't make a whole heck of a lot of money on hot sauce and Bloody Mary mix — they account for maybe 2 percent of our total annual sales — but I love that they're another facet of the business and help the business to grow.

That kind of expansion and creative branding is exciting and rewarding, but Bobbie Weiner Enterprises is a makeup company first and always will be.

Chapter 12

Getting Out There, Giving Back

By the mid-2000s, Bobbie Weiner Enterprises was thriving. My team and I were focused on new product development, growing sales and of course — promotion, promotion, promotion!

I kept up a steady pace of conventions and shows, dotting the country and racking up "frequent flyer" airline miles each time. Once we acquired enough distributors, we discontinued the smaller shows. But still, every spring I hit the road for about four shows in three weeks' time. The biggest shows we do each year are for the military and the haunt industry; those industries became the bread and butter of our business. We also starting appearing at an annual "shot show" for the hunting industry and supply a lot of camouflage for hunters now.

I found an agent and got bookings all over the country for my "Makeup to Die For" seminars, in which I taught special effects makeup to everyone from high school and college students to haunted house professionals. (My lessons on how to give a seminar years earlier were now paying off!)

I have always believed that no matter how big the company gets, I need to stay out in front. If people don't see the face behind the name of the company, they'll think you're out of business — or dead.

We created a Bloody Mary fan club that helped our new and long-time customers keep up with our burgeoning company. To be a member, people would pay $10, they would get a pair of fangs and a monthly newsletter. They also would get a 10 percent discount on products.

The fan club grew quickly, and today "Dear Bloody Mary's" Fan Club has over 1,000 members around the world. The fan club has a president in San Francisco who now writes the monthly newsletter for me. She also comes with me to all the shows, so people know who she is. She's great at letting people know where I'm going and what I'm doing.

And then there's the event I look more forward to than anything else all year — the Bloody Mary Cruise. Carnival Cruise Lines came to me in 2001 and proposed a Bloody Mary-themed cruise around Halloween. I agreed to do makeup and workshops on a cruise the week after Halloween that year, but then 9/11 happened, and all plans got scrapped.

I figured I probably could put a Bloody Mary cruise together myself — why not? How hard could it be? — and we set sail for the first time in January 2003 with 58 people in our group. We haven't missed a cruise since then, one year even having 110 passengers on board. We now embark on Super Bowl Sunday and head to the Caribbean for 7 days on a Royal Caribbean cruise line. These are a great time; forget formal-wear for dinner. Our group really dresses up (usually I'm a nun). The next cruise will be my 9th one, and we're bringing in a guest speaker so that people from the haunt industry can write it off as a business trip!

I started private labeling for people, and this was something entirely new. No one else would private label camouflage makeup until I came along. I don't care if my name's not on it – what do I care as long as I get their check? I trusted my instincts — once again, when I got an idea, I ran with it. We also drop-ship our products anywhere, to anyone. So if someone starts an Ebay business and needs Bloody Mary makeup, to sell, we'll drop-ship it direct to the consumers.

We now have Bloody Mary makeup consultants all over the country who sell our face paint and other products through direct sales parties. But unlike most of these kinds of makeup consultants, ours aren't selling for beauty; they're selling death makeup or theatrical makeup for zombies and vampires and all manner of "haunt" creatures.

ೲ ೲ ೲ ೲ ೲ

Once the business took off, I made charity work a huge priority — especially for the military and for children.

At the urging of my friends, the wrestlers in the WWE, I started flying around the country visiting Army bases. My friend John, the WWE marketing manager, had noticed at Fort Hood in Texas that the PX carried a huge counter display of my camouflage. Some of the wrestlers, including "Stone Cold" Steve Austin, were there signing autographs.

"Hey, there's Bobbie's camo," John commented.

"Who is that?" the PX manager asked?

John explained that I supplied all the camo for the government and that I was a friend of his. The manager asked him if I'd consider making an appearance there and paint children's faces, and John got me on the phone immediately. A month later, I was on a plane to Fort Hood, where I painted kids' faces for eight hours straight and autographed all kinds of Bloody Mary stuff. I have made a few visits to Fort Hood, as well as to Fort Bragg in North Carolina and Fort Lewis in Washington state.

I also started painting kids' faces at the military's annual Snowball Express event. This one's always tough to do, emotionally, because it's for children who have had a parent die in service to the country. Doing face-painting for hours at a time is no small task. Sure, I could hire an assistant, but when "the lady from Titanic" is there, the kids want "the lady from Titanic" to do their faces!

Once at a charity event, six clowns had been hired to help me face-paint. None of the kids were jumping in line for them; they were all coming to me. The kids were scared of the clowns and didn't want to go near them! Happy to help but a bit stressed out, I said to the clowns, "Go take off your makeup! You're scaring the kids!" They refused, saying, "We are clowns. We're not taking our makeup off." So it was another long day of face-painting.

Little kids, by the way, call me "Mary." They always say, "There's not really a Bloody Mary, is there?" And I say no, it's make-believe, because they're scared of the idea of a bloody woman named Mary!

Once the kids get a little bit older, though, they start to love Bloody Mary!

In 2007 we licensed the name Bloody Mary and our 5th comic book theme to the Six Flags over Texas Theme Park in Arlington, Texas, and "Bloody Mary's Circus of Fear" Haunted Atraction was born. We give all proceeds to the Boy Scouts. Universal Studios theme park also approached us and wanted to use the name Bloody Mary for a haunted house — "Halloween Horror Nights from Bloody Mary." It's a huge Halloween attraction now!

Chapter 13

New Places, New Faces

In 2007, I said to Tom, "Let's get out of Florida. I don't like hurricanes and it is time to move."

He and his wife were ready, and I was weary of commuting to California from Florida. When Tom said there was no way he would move to California, I gave him a choice: "Colorado or Texas," I said. "Your pick."

He chose Texas, the Dallas/Fort Worth area, with good schools and great housing. I flew to Texas and found a warehouse and office, got Tom and his family a place to live and found a home for myself. Relieved that I would be a lot closer to Los Angeles and San Diego, we moved one month later. I made another overnight move, while Tom drove across country with his family.

So I became a cowgirl. Another experience. Tom and his wife have met some great friends, and love the school their daughter attends. I've also made wonderful friendships, and Texas is now home base for my corporation. I'm a long way from Beverly Hills, and profoundly grateful for the opportunities that have led me to this new home.

Since I picked up and moved to Texas, life has not slowed down in the least. I continued to work 6 or 7 days a week, still married to my company. Each year, we develop quirky new products, from spray-blood to tattoo cover kits to "living statue" makeup kits. And I continue to get noticed for the crazy little business I run.

In the summer of 2009, I appeared on the recently-launched Joan Rivers show called How'd You Get so Rich? This experience was a hoot-and-a-half, starting with the fact that I turned it down initially. Producers from Mark Burnett Productions had called me after they saw me on the Donny Deutch show The Big Idea.

Their timing was awful: I had just landed in Orlando for the big Shot Show, one of my biggest shows of the year. Tom called to let me know that Mark Burnett's people contacted him about me going on the show. I was so confused. I only knew Mark Burnett from the reality show Survivor.

"You're kidding! The people who eat worms?" I asked. "What do they want with me? I hate bugs."

I had no intention of going on Survivor, but I called them back anyway.

The woman said, "We want you to fly here to New York to meet with us — tomorrow."

I said, "I can't."

She said, "Do you know who we are?"

I said, "Yeah! But, do you know who I AM? I just showed up at the Shot Show, and I have an appointment with The Israeli Army tomorrow."

This was no lie. The next day I was meeting with the Israeli military reps about supplying camouflage face paint.

She wouldn't take no for an answer. She called back the same afternoon and announced they would have a crew coming to me — at the Shot Show, in Orlando — the next day. Sure enough, the next day I met with the Israeli Department of Defense and then I met with Mark Burnett's television producers.

Two months later, I was on the show.

They offered to shoot it at my home in Texas and I said no — I'm a single woman; I didn't want my house on TV! Next they wanted to shoot it at my production facility in Long Beach and I said no; my business is none of their business!

Finally they tried to get me to go back to the Bel Air home I shared with my ex-husband; they thought it would evoke some emotion from me. (They knew it was; they'd already found it.) I said no way — I wasn't going back there.

Joan Rivers herself called to help figure out how to make my show appearance happen. They were only doing six shows in the series, and I was basically the only woman they were going to feature. She wanted to make it happen. I agreed to fly out to California to do the show in March and suggested we shoot inside a limousine and drive around. They added that I should be coming out of the hoity-toity Louis Lacari salon, having just had my hair done. (They really did make me straighten my always-curly hair for the show, too.) I also was supposed to wear black and be dripping with diamonds. Well, anyone who knows me knows my usual work attire is a Bloody Mary sweatshirt, jeans and a cowboy hat; I don't own diamonds! I went out and got a black suit and a bunch of fake jewelry for the show.

The night before the show taped, I was supposed to go to dinner with Joan. But that's the day actress Natasha Richardson died in a skiing accident, and Joan – a good friend of Natasha and her husband, actor Liam Neeson, went on Larry King Live instead. So we postponed our meal until the next day.

Being with Joan on the set was marvelous. Between takes, we'd talk about life and I got to know her as a human being. It took a full day to film my segment. On the first take, Joan "stopped me" coming out of the salon and asked how much I'd "paid" to get my hair done by Louis Lacari. I had no idea what that place actually cost. I said $200. They said "cut." They told me to say $700, so that's what I said on the next take.

Then I jumped in a limo with Joan Rivers, and she asked me how much my company was worth. Again, I had no idea. She said to say "30 million dollars" — so I did. (I WISH my company were worth that! Ha, in my dreams!)

Joan and I shared a meal together and discovered that we had been neighbors when I lived in Bel Air! She was such a nice person with a great sense of humor. I also got to know her hard-working makeup artist, who I came to admire a lot; I'm still in touch with her today. She considers me a hero because I stopped out of the Hollywood box and did something different. I'm still in touch with the woman who did my hair for the show, too. It's incredible how many people come into my life like that and we bond. The whole experience with the show was wonderful.

ᔧᔤ ᔧᔤ ᔧᔤ ᔧᔤ ᔧᔤ

Early on, I felt my Sport Fan Face Paint would be a great fit for fast food restaurants. I called and wrote them all, but no one responded until 2009. Taco Bells and Pizza Huts in Minnesota started selling my face paint for the Vikings and Brett Favre, bless him, who joined the Vikings that same year. Minnesota was the flagship state, and other teams will follow suit when energetic sports fans clamor for my paint kits.

If you watched the 2010 World Cup in South Africa on television and saw fans in the stands wearing face paint, it was ours, too. Bobbie Weiner Enterprises supplied face paint for all of the teams during the weeks-long tournament. On the wall of my office, I still have a calendar

I found that contained the flags of every country around the world, so that I could study the colors for all the teams.

ﻌﻌﻌ ﻌﻌﻌ ﻌﻌﻌ ﻌﻌﻌ ﻌﻌﻌ

We're still supplying makeup that gets used on TV. In 2010, our products were used on the hit ABC show Extreme Makeover: Home Edition. This one featured a "haunted house makeover" at the Oregon School for the Deaf in Salem, Oregon.

We had sponsored the school at a haunted house convention the year before. Then, when I found out they got the Extreme Makeover, I called the head of the school and asked if they would need makeup. He gave the Extreme Makeover people my name, and they called me and asked me for a lot of blood. I also offered dirt, zombie makeup and other haunted house staples, and we shipped them out to them. The folks from the show asked me to fly out for the "big reveal" on the show, but I was unable to make it out there in time.

ﻌﻌﻌ ﻌﻌﻌ ﻌﻌﻌ ﻌﻌﻌ ﻌﻌﻌ

Bobbie Weiner Enterprises continues to gain an international presence. In 2010, I was a guest speaker for the International Makeup Artists Trade Show in Sydney, Australia. We have a lot of accounts in the United Kingdom and in New Zealand, too.

Some of my distributors in Australia are working to set up a showroom in Hong Kong! I'm especially excited about this marvelous opportunity and can't wait until it opens in 2012.

And we now supply camouflage face paint to armed forces from China to Sweden, from Colombia to Canada.

However, no matter how high-profile Bobbie Weiner Enterprises gets around the world, it remains a little business, run out of a small office in Fort Worth, Texas. We're not Maybelline or Estee Lauder or even Mary Kay. They don't sell what I sell, and vice versa. I'm not out to steal their business, and they'll never compete in our world, either.

I spend a significant amount of time mixing up blood in my tiny "blood room" at the office, and from July to October, we have 50 gallons ready to be shipped out any time, any place. The days are unpredictable; sometimes the fax machine tells us how busy we'll be filling orders and shipping products.

I have a wonderful team working around me each day, and our products continue to evolve. I go to bed each night with a legal pad and a pen, and usually by the morning, I've written down a new idea to try. Tom and I strive to make "Tales of Bloody Mary" better with each issue, and we continue to come up with new ways to get the name out there. We have a great working relationship, and we've been at it so long, we're like an old married couple now — well, except one half of the couple is married to the business, and that's me!

We were fortunate in that we weren't hit terribly hard by the economic downturn of recent years. Camouflage, now, is basically 80 percent of our business. But we're always selling something. If we're not selling camo, we're selling Sports Fan face paint. If we're not selling that, we're selling Halloween face paint. We're diversified enough to always be hitting one segment or another.

Halloween, as anyone could imagine, is HUGE for us each year, and starts in July. People know that I make the makeup here in this country so they don't need to order it too far in advance. I can't really compete with the companies who make face paint kits in China and sell them in grocery stores for $1.99. There's a reason they're so cheap. They're the ones that say, "don't get this near your eyes, don't get near your mouth." I don't put that on my makeup. Mine doesn't have lead or animal fats or other junk in it; it's not going hurt anybody. I'm proud of our quality, and it will never change as long as my name is on it.

In July and August, our Internet sales go nuts. We package blood at least 5 different ways and we make 31 different kits, and up until midnight on October 31 every year, we are Fed-Exing this stuff like crazy. Hey, if a customer wants to pay 40 bucks to have a $7.99-product shipped overnight the day before Halloween, we'll do it.

In the years ahead, I'm thinking of establishing a makeup scholarship for students who have the passion, drive and talent to excel in the field that — I'm quite sure — saved my own life.

Epilogue

When I was a little girl, I dreamed of being famous. I didn't really know what I wanted to "do" when I grew up, mind you, but I would tell my mother, "I want to be famous some day." (Not surprisingly, this declaration met with little response.)

Thank goodness I dreamed bigger. I don't want to be famous anymore — yes, I have achieved some bit of limelight for both my business and my work in Hollywood. But marketing is different from fame.

I want to pay my bills. I want to make quality products. I want to continue running a successful business with integrity. Fame doesn't necessarily buy you any of those things.

The kind of "fan mail" I get now are letters from customers who thank me for treating them with respect, for taking time to help them with their needs and for taking pride in my business. That's not fame; it's recognition for a job well done, and it's so much sweeter.

I lived in the fancy house near movie stars in L.A. — the kind that had people on the street asking, "I wonder who lives in THAT house?" Well, you know what, I lived there and it wasn't that great. It was a house of cards that crumbled all around me.

What defines us is what we become after we fall.

People may say, "If your ex could see you now!" But, OK — look at me now. There are people who have a lot more than I do and people who have a lot less. Does that really matter?

The bottom line is we are all just living life, and sometimes we have to figure out what to do when "life" happens to us.

You get up in the morning, you eat breakfast, you go to work, you go home at night, you eat dinner, you watch TV and you go to bed. And in between all that, what have you accomplished? Are you leaving a positive mark? Are you making people happy? Are you offering the world something just a little bit unique?

I have made some enormous sacrifices to ensure my company's success: I went years without my own home and even sold my car when I was desperate. For the second half of my adult life, I've lived alone with my cat, who doesn't mind that I'm in a long-term relationship with my business. And I never had children, which is my biggest regret.

But I still count myself among the lucky people of the world.

At a point of loss and heartbreak, I discovered kind and generous people. In the face of rejection and fear, I set my sights on success. With every step and misstep, I learned something useful. And I proved that I can do this!

I wish anyone who reads this book the opportunity to fulfill his or her own aspirations. Pursue those dreams with honesty, integrity and passion.

You CAN do it, too!

Bobbie's 12 Tips For Success

1. Say yes ... and then figure out how to do it.

Obviously I believe in this principle, or I wouldn't have titled the book I Can Do This! This practice has been a pattern throughout my life, and bedrock to my success. I didn't know how to dress a dollhouse with blood to look like a slaughterhouse, but I said yes and figured out to do it, got the nickname Bloody Mary — and it changed my life. I didn't know the first thing about colleges' school colors, but I took orders for those colleges anyway, figured it out, and it changed my life. I didn't know how to make camouflage paint, but I said yes to the Marines, figured out how to do it — and it changed my life.

I have never let a lack of understanding or resources be obstacles to getting the job done. When I was figuring out how to get military orders, I spent all day on the phone, racking up a $400 phone bill, gathering information about which codes I needed. When I needed money for my business and banks wouldn't give me a loan, I sold my car. And when I needed a new car and didn't have the money, I showed them my orders and negotiated a deal to come back later with the money.

The people who are the most successful in their careers (or in any endeavors, from running the kids' PTA to running a marathon) are those who can see past, around or through obstacles to keep their goals in sight.

Find the confidence to accept a challenge, and then figure out how to achieve it. More times than not, the payoff will be worth it in the end.

2. Never let age be an obstacle.

You're truly not done in life until you're dead. People break the wedding vow "till death do us part" all the time, but make that same vow to your dreams — and then keep it!

My father always said, "You're put on this earth and you have choices." So maybe you screwed up some of those choices early in life — or, as in my case with my marriage, someone else made choices that screwed up my life...or so I thought at the time. But the great thing is that we always get another day to make another choice to live a more fulfilled life. It sounds cliché, but it's true — with age comes wisdom.

I started makeup school in my 40s and quickly became known as the old lady in the Hollywood makeup trailers. Sometimes this worked to my advantage, though, because producers would rely on me to help keep the actors' heads on straight. Older actresses hired me for regular jobs because they trusted me and liked the way I did their makeup, more than the younger artists.

I started my business when I was already "middle aged." Most people, by the time they're 50, are thinking toward retirement. I was thinking of how to get the money I needed to embark on this new and maybe-not-so-crazy idea I had for a company. I was dreaming new dreams for myself, and the reality became bigger and better than I could ever have imagined.

Keep dreaming, keep working, and if you're "getting up there in age," you have a resource that the young people doing the same thing don't have — past experiences to draw on and learn from. Use them to your advantage. I guarantee you won't repeat the mistakes you've most learned from, and you'll use them to achieve even more than you set out to do. I sure did!

3. Always keep yourself fresh.

Keep the ideas coming. Don't allow yourself to be dormant. Allow one possibility, and one idea, to lead to another. When you find something you love to do, keep finding ways to have fun with it.

I have to reinvent myself constantly. I've always had an entrepreneurial spirit, and I've always had to keep moving. I would never, ever be happy at a desk job, and my life would have been miserable had I chosen a career path that required me to wear a suit to the office every day. I had a desk job for two weeks once. In my first year of college, my father's best friend, who was a lawyer, hired me to do administrative work in his office. I could not read my shorthand, and I generally was an office screw-up. After two weeks of this disastrous situation, that was it. Then I started my thrift shop.

Now when I walk into the office each morning, I never know what's going to happen. I don't know how busy we'll be or where we'll be shipping products. The fax machine might start going crazy with orders from the Army, or I might have to quickly drop-ship an overnight order the week before Halloween. I love to be kept on my toes; I love the challenge of the unknown.

I travel as many weeks out of the year as I'm home these days, so I have a lot of time on airplanes. Whether it's the near-silence in the cabin or the fact that my phone has to be turned off, I end up getting a flood of ideas on these flights and scribbling them on scraps of paper. I wrote the first draft of this book on airplanes. I even just wrote a musical on airplanes (stay tuned!) At work I just started experimenting with spray-blood that spritzes from a tube; it's selling like crazy. Now THAT's not something I ever thought I'd be doing 20 years ago!

Find yourself a niche and then be creative. You have to be really cautious, but you also have to take risks to reap any rewards down the road. You can't care what people think too much; you just have to go for it. If my old Beverly Hills tennis-girlfriends could see me in my office every day, mixing blood in the "blood room," they'd fall over in hysterics. Who cares?

If you find a niche and set a goal, just figure out how to achieve it … because nobody's going to do it for you.

4. Be willing to work for cheap — and work just as hard as you would if you were making a lot of money. The contacts and experience will prove to be priceless.

I now own a company that makes a lot of money, but there is not a day when I work harder or feel more motivated than I did when I arrived on the Pumpkinhead II set, making up actors' grotesque faces for just $35.

Had I passed up that first opportunity out of makeup school, I firmly believe, I would not be where I am today. If you connect the dots of my career, they all trace back to that single job. After all, that's when "Bloody Mary" was born.

Let's be realistic here. One of the reasons I could afford to work for near nothing back then is that I still had some money left from my divorce and I only had myself to support. Other people had turned down the Pumpkinhead II gig before I was called; it's possible that they absolutely could not afford to work for such little money. I could, and I jumped at the chance.

Taking a low-paying job or a nonpaid internship may not be an option if you have a family to feed. But if you can find a way to do it, and take advantage of the invaluable learning experiences it will provide, I am living proof that it can change your life in unimaginable ways.

5. Persistence pays off.

As they say, slow and steady wins the race. When I was in makeup school, I wasn't the most talented student — not by a long shot. But you'd better believe I worked harder than the other students put together. I stayed for hours after class, studying the training tapes no one else did.

Years later, the director of the school, Tate Holland, would continue to use my experience as an example to his students. In a newsletter sent to the Los Angeles School of Makeup students and alumni, he said, "If there is one common component that I have noticed in successful makeup artists … it would be persistence. Persistence over talent, persistence over contacts, persistence over money.

"My favorite story on this subject," he says, "is about a friend of mine and former student named Bobbie Weiner. The first thing I noticed about Bobbie was not her talent as a makeup artist but her positive attitude, enthusiasm and persistence. This lady could not be beat; whether it was a technique that she had trouble mastering in class or working her first non-paid job as a makeup artist, Bobbie persisted."

If you have a goal in mind, persist until you achieve it. Resist the temptation to compare yourself to other people, feel defeated and throw in the towel. It might take years down the road, but at some point, your persistence WILL pay off.

6. If you think you have a good idea, take the steps to own it — legally.

I owe this one to my father, too. As soon as I put my name on my first makeup product, he told me to hire an attorney and trademark it. I trademarked my own name and my nickname, Bloody Mary, and now they're all over my products — and only MY products.

My attorney laughed when I told him I wanted to trademark "Bloody Mary" Bloody Mary mix; he didn't really think it could be done. But guess what — I did it anyway, and now I am the only one who can stamp a bottle with "Bloody Mary Bloody Mary mix."

Now if anyone tries to use my name or nickname on their own products (as another high-profile entrepreneur did recently with "Bloody Mary"), I can take legal action to stop them. It can be expensive, yes. But this is simple self-preservation, and it is crucial to building your own business.

I learned this lesson the hard way before I launched my own business, when a "friend" hired me to come up with some new concepts for the publishing company for which he was a marketing rep. Through that bad experience, I learned that if you don't somehow get your name on your product, you'll lose control — and profits — very quickly. Somebody's going to steal it.

The business world is full of scammers. Lessen your chances of being duped and cheated by making sure you own your brand.

7. Surround yourself with good people.

By that, I mean people who will help you succeed, who have your back, and with whom you share mutual respect. No one can run a successful business alone. It takes a good, solid support team to truly excel. Bobbie Weiner Enterprises wouldn't be what it is today without the great people — like my artist Tom Carlton — who help me every day.

If you're a manager, you've got to be a team player, but you must still be a leader. The difference between a herd and a mob is that a herd has a leader and a mob is unruly. You want to be the leader of a herd, but be clear on your expectations for your employees, or there WILL be a mob scene — even if the people you manage are good, nice people.

In your everyday life — whether at work or after hours — make the conscious decision to be around people who will enhance your life. If they're not enhancing your life, don't go near them because they're going to suck you dry. I have dumped a lot of people along the way because they were sapping my energy, and for no good reason.

Also, if you get a gut feeling that someone you meet is going to use you, you're probably right. Don't be friends with these kinds of obsequious people; you'll never get away from their attempts to use and abuse you. A lot of times, these kinds of people don't even know they're users. I can't tell you the number of people who have tried to utilize my connections to Hollywood, or have asked me to donate my time or money or products, never to give me anything in return. I'm happy to help people and donate to good causes, but if I get an inkling that that's all a person wants me for, I'm outta there.

8. Don't be shy about getting out in front of people to get ahead.

When I came back from the Titanic set and launched my business, I contacted every media outlet I could reach in my area. I was no dummy. I knew the cache that a Titanic movie credit would give me, and I would have been foolish not to use that to my advantage in promoting myself and my business. Sure enough — I got the first military contract for camouflage because a bigwig with the Marines was watching my appearance on a morning television show. Stories about me in the newspaper led to speaking engagements, which led to further promotion of my business.

I used this same "get out there and grab them" approach each time I set up a booth at a trade show, from using real butterflies at a book fair, to luring customers with a popcorn machine at a military show.

If you're a business owner, you should be your own biggest promoter. I've never had to have a marketing or public relations manager; I've always jumped head first into promotions by myself. After all, I'm the name and face of my company – why shouldn't I?

9. All mistakes are golden.

Making mistakes is how you learn. I made a lot of mistakes, and I'm still making mistakes today. I look back now on what I've learned from them, and I'm a wiser person. People say, "if I only knew then what I know now." But life doesn't work that way. You only know now what you know now; it doesn't work backwards.

Every day is a new day. It's a chance to make better choices and do things better, but it's not a "do over." Don't beat yourself up for mistakes or poor choices you made yesterday. What's the point? If we did that, I'd never stop punishing myself and asking what I could have done differently early on in my life.

The sun doesn't rise on a new day each morning so that we can spend the next 23 hours atoning for the mistakes we made the day before. The sun comes up, and the sun sets, and in the hours in between, we do the best we can to move forward, using the wisdom we gained from days gone by.

One more thing about mistakes: again, I'm no marriage counselor here, but no marriage is perfect. Of course there are people who are happy and in love and have been married 40 years. But there's no perfect marriage. It's unfair to expect your spouse to be perfect. There's no perfect anything.

You're perfect when you're dead because you can't make any mistakes.

10. Make sure you can take care of yourself.

Women, I'm mostly talking to you, and I'm talking from personal experience. Don't give up who you are. You must have an identity all your own.

In my young adulthood, I ran a really successful thrift shop; I made decent money and got a lot of respect from my employees, customers and community. My first three marriages came and went, but I still feel like I knew who I was. And then, along came Dr. Perfect. I quickly became "The Doctor's Wife." Sure, I still raised money for charity, but I did it as "The Doctor's Wife." I hung out at the country club and played tennis as "The Doctor's Wife." Well guess what, when the doctor left, so did all the rest of that — most importantly, my identity.

To the core of my being, I no longer knew who I was without him. I had absolutely no life of my own anymore. As soon as he'd put a ring on my finger, I'd put on a new identity, too. Too many women think the words "I do" and "I am" are the same thing. They are not.

I was The Doctor's Wife. Now I am Bloody Mary — and it's so much better.

Again, I don't pretend to be an expert on marriage (God knows I got four chances and couldn't get it right), but I know a lot about reinventing yourself. And in order to keep your own identity when you get married, you must bring something to the table; you must have your own life. Have your own career or at least pursue your own interests — things that take you out of the house, into the real world where you meet interesting people and have great stories to share around the dinner table at night. Grab the ring and be a part of the show.

There's another part of maintaining your identity during marriage, and that has to do with dollars and cents (and sense)! Again, I'm not going to tell you how to run your marriage, but keep this in mind: if you let someone else pay the bills, they own you. If you're not out there working and bringing money to the table — and this is no disdain for hardworking stay-at-home moms — at the very least, know where the money goes in your household. Know how much is coming in and going out, and resist the temptation to let your husband do all the bookkeeping and pay all the bills. There truly was no worse time in my life than when my husband disappeared,when I had to figure out how to pay all our expenses and keep a roof over my own head. I don't wish that kind of pain and grief and helplessness on any other woman in the world.

11. Remember that someone is always living a less fortunate life than you. Do your part to give back.

Throughout my life, I've been rich and I've been poor; rich is better. I've driven Porsches, and I've driven a tiny rental car; Porsches are better. But the good thing about going through a financial hard time is that it truly does make you appreciate all the other good things you have in your life. I can honestly say I wouldn't trade a moment of my life — rich or poor.

Whether you are driven by karma or just a natural instinct to make people happy, if you're going to be truly successful AND happy in life, you must give back to those with a need. My mother always said, "give once, and it's always going to give back double or triple."

Helping those in need doesn't necessarily mean giving handouts to people on the side of the road or attending high-dollar benefit galas (which you may or may not really be able to afford anyway).

Again, find a niche, a unique way to give back. I've always been drawn to charities that help children, since the days I ran a thrift shop that benefited kids with cancer. These days, my haunted house each Halloween gives 100 percent of proceeds to the Boy Scouts. We donate makeup like crazy to other charity haunted houses around town.

I face-paint for hundreds of kids at Snowball Express, the armed forces' annual fundraiser extravaganza for kids whose parents have died in military service to the country. And every year, I also face paint for Give Kids the World, for children who are suffering from a terminal illness and only have about a year to live. This one in particular is really meaningful to me. I've been blessed and lucky to have a long, amazing life, and I feel compelled to do something nice for kids whose lives will be cut short. I always come back feeling very emotional after that event.

I've spoken to high schools and colleges, too, and people e-mail to let me know how much my story inspires them.

Think about the unique gifts and talents you have, and how you can use them to give back to those less fortunate. I guarantee you will make someone else feel like a million bucks — and you'll feel like it yourself!

12. Above all else, be a nice person.

"You don't judge a book by its cover." That's another lesson that my father taught me early on; he didn't just say it, he made me live it. I think it's one reason why, in my 20s, I was so successful at running a thrift shop. I didn't know who was going to walk through the door and how much money they had in their pocket. And I didn't care; I treated everyone the same, as my father had taught me years ago. There are almost no shades of gray; people are either scammers or they're nice people, he'd say.

My father set the bar high. An accomplished and honorable business man, Dad always said to me, "If you are a nice person and become successful, you will be an even nicer person. If you are a no-good bastard and become successful, you will more than likely be a bigger no-good bastard." It's the choices we make — including in how we conduct ourselves — that define us.

Also, be positive. People like to be around positive people, not negative people. (Remember the old saying "You attract more bees with honey?") When you get out of bed in the morning, you've got a 50-50 chance whether it's gonna be a good day or a bad day. And I never want a bad day. I haven't had a bad day in a long time. I don't have time to even think about negativity. Every day I will pull something good out of it.

Finally, be humble. People respond to humility. Remember where you came from and how you achieved your success. If you have always been humble, don't stop once the success starts. If you don't have humility, try to find some.

If for no other reason, be humble for this reason: you never, EVER know which contacts and connections may lead to future opportunities and successes. I'm living proof of that!

Bobbie in her first Office (Her Bedroom)

Bobbie with a Frozen Make Up Model

Bobbie's First Camouflage Face Paint Convention

Bobbie in her 1st Sports Fan Booth

Bobbie Painting Seth with Sports Fan Face Paint

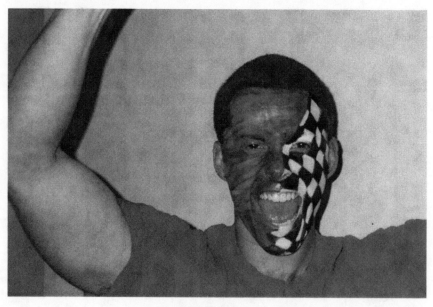

Guy with Racing Face Paint

Bobbie with Black Hawk Unit

Bobbie receiving a Gold Medal for her Face Paint

Bobbie with a Vampire

ESPN Commercial

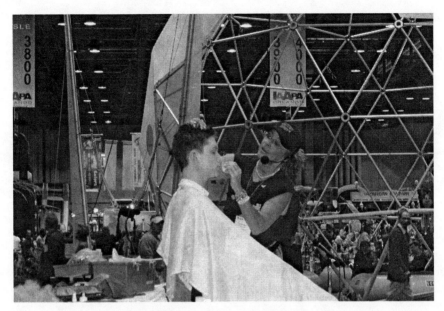

IAAPA Stage Demo

MCRD Face painting the kids

San Diego Chargers Game

World Series - Face Painting Kids

The 1st Comic Book reached the stores

Bobbie at a Horror Convention

Comic Con 06 Fans in line for Autographs

Comic Con 06 Bobbie Weiner and Tom Carlton with Fan

Bobbie Weiner with Tom Carlton at The Fiery Food Show 2011

Bloody Mary Cruise Group

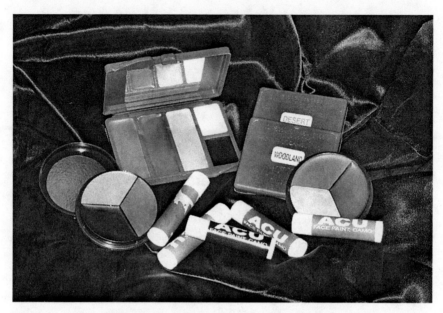

Camouflage Face Paint Makeup Line

Bloody Mary Makeup Line

About the Author

Bobbie Weiner resides in Dallas/Fort Worth with her big old cat, Camouflage. She is currently concocting her annual Bloody Mary Halloween Horror Cruise. She continues to license her fifth comic book, Tales of Bloody Mary –The Circus of Fear, to Fright Fest at Six Flags Over Texas. All proceeds are donated to the Boy Scouts of America. Bobbie has licensed her name, Bloody Mary, to Universal Studios, Orlando, for Halloween Horror Night.

CPSIA information can be obtained at www.ICGtesting.com
Printed in the USA
LVOW041325071111

253869LV00001BA/3/P